GREEN CITY DEVELOPMENT TOOL KIT

ADB

ASIAN DEVELOPMENT BANK

© 2015 Asian Development Bank
6 ADB Avenue, Mandaluyong City, 1550 Metro Manila, Philippines
Tel +63 2 632 4444; Fax +63 2 636 2444
www.adb.org; openaccess.adb.org

Some rights reserved. Published in 2015.
Printed in the Philippines.

ISBN 978-92-9257-012-5 (Print), 978-92-9257-013-2 (e-ISBN)
Publication Stock No. TIM146861

Cataloging-In-Publication Data

Asian Development Bank.
        Green city development tool kit
Mandaluyong City, Philippines: Asian Development Bank, 2015.

1. Cities.   2. Urban development.   3. Sustainable Development.   4. Environment.   5. Asia.
I. Asian Development Bank.

Contents

Tables, Figures, and Boxes

TABLES

FIGURES

BOXES

Abbreviations

3E	Economy, environment, and equity
ADB	Asian Development Bank
BOO	build-own-operate
BOOT	build-own-operate-transfer
BREEAM	Building Research Establishment Environmental Assessment Method
CCA	Climate Change Adaptation
CCC	Committee on Climate Change
CCAS	Climate Change Adaptation Strategy
CDIA	Cities Development Initiative for Asia
CE	Circle Economy
CIRIA	Construction Industry Research and Information Association
CO_2	carbon dioxide
CDM	Clean Development Mechanism
DBOM	design–build–operate–maintain
Defra	Department for Environment and Rural Affairs
DMC	developing member country
DRR	Disaster Risk Reduction
EE	energy efficiency
EFFECT	Energy Forecasting Framework and Emissions Consensus Tool
ESMAP	Energy Sector Management Assistance Program
GDP	gross domestic product
GEF	Global Environment Facility
GHG	greenhouse gas
GPWM	Global Partnership for Waste Management
ICLEI	International Council for Local Environmental Initiatives (ICLEI-Local Governments for Sustainability)
IPCC	Intergovernmental Panel on Climate Change
ISWMP	Integrated Solid Waste Management Plan
IWRM	Integrated Water Resource Management
IUWM	Integrated Urban Water Management
LCLIP	Local Climate Impact Profile
LEED	Leadership in Energy and Environmental Design
LSE	London School of Economics
MSWM	Municipal Solid Waste Management
NGO	nongovernment organization
PPP	public–private partnership
RACE	Rapid Assessment of City Emissions
REEEP	Renewal Energy and Energy Efficiency Partnerships
SuDS	Sustainable Drainage Systems
TEEMP	Transport Emissions Evaluation Models for Projects
TOD	Transit Oriented Development
TRACE	Tool for Rapid Assessment of City Energy
UCCR	Urban Climate Change Resilience

UKCIP	United Kingdom Climate Impacts Programme
UNEP	United Nations Environment Programme
UOP	Urban Operational Plan
WB	World Bank
WHO	World Health Organization
WSP	Water and Sanitation Program
WSSCC	Water Supply and Sanitation Collaborative Council

Acknowledgments

This tool kit was written by Emma Lewis (ICF) and inputs and discussion of colleagues provided during the preparation of this document are gratefully acknowledged. The author would like to thank ADB Sustainable Development and Climate Change Department (SDCC) for their support of this initiative.

Thank you to retired Lead Urban Development Expert, Michael Lindfield, for his early comments and guidance and Jingmin Huang for her insightful comments and support during the preparation of this document. Grateful acknowledgment also to CEPT University for their preparatory inputs and to Royston Brockman (ICF) and Jose Monroy (ICF) for their support and comments.

Thank you for all the instructive feedback received from the Urban Sector Group (USG), specifically the invaluable comments from Alexandra Vogl, Antoine Morel, Sonia Chand Sandhu, Arghya Singha, Srinivas Sampath, Satoshi Ishii, Ramola Naik Sangu and Florian Steinberg.

Editing was done by the Department of External Relations Publishing and Dissemination Team. Vergel Latay assisted with editorial matters and provided overall coordination of production and publication.

Preface

This is a reference guide (herein called the tool kit) for Asian Development Bank (ADB) staff and consultants, and city leaders that introduces key concepts of Green City development and identifies crosscutting issues. It outlines a three-step city assessment framework and provides a summary of existing tools and resources for green and sustainable development. Users of the tool kit will gain a greater understanding of key issues for green city development that will assist in the preparation and design of green city development programs and projects in Asian cities.

Asia is urbanizing rapidly. It is predicted that from 2015, population growth in Asia will predominantly occur in urban centers.[1] Pressure on resources and increased demand on local and global environments, coupled with the need and expectation to improve the overall quality of life of residents, means that now, more than ever, the decisions taken by governments (across all levels) and its populace have never been more important. How Asian cities respond to these challenges has local, regional, and international reach.

Cities are dynamic and complex. Defining what a *Green City* is will mean, and does mean, many different things to different people. There is no universal solution that can be applied to every city in any country. Adaptable, responsive, and innovative solutions that differ from one place to another enable Green Cities to emerge in various guises and recognize the variation and dynamism of cities. This tool kit examines green city development and the tools that are available to assist ADB staff and consultants in developing and designing urban programs to support cities develop in a green and sustainable manner.

Building on the concept of integrated development planning and a "system-based" approach, this tool kit introduces the principles of sustainable urban development, highlights crosscutting themes and recognizes the interconnection of sectors and the importance of sequencing. It also recognizes that cities will evolve to different levels of "green" at varying rates and that this development is not uniform.

Reflecting the three main stages (preparation/scoping, design, and evaluation) of any project or program, available tools, resources, and links are identified by relevant categories. These have also been set out by sector and theme—water, solid waste, transport, energy, the built environment, climate change adaptation, disaster risk reduction, and urban (general). A detailed summary (see Chapter 4) of each is provided, sign posting users to crosscutting themes and where to find relevant additional resources.

The complex nature of cities, the vast amount of information available, and pressure to "do more with less" create an environment that, within the context of *Green City* development, is challenging. It is often difficult for decision makers to prioritize green investment when pressure for resources may be more pronounced in other more immediate areas and provision of basic services. As such, green city development cannot focus only on the physical manifestation of "green" development but needs to include sustained education and support to capacity building both at the community and institutional levels—thus supporting behavior change and prioritizing green development initiatives.

---

[1]   M. Lindfield and F. Steinberg, eds. 2012. *Green Cities*. Manila: Asian Development Bank.

The early stages of sustainability and environmental management from the early 1990s and the Agenda 21 platform that sought to integrate these principles into city planning and development processes have evolved. Sustainability and environmental management techniques are still framed within the three main categories of environment, social, and economic but have evolved to also now include climate change mitigation and adaptation, resilient communities, and responding to disaster risk. Further, the metrics for calculating potential impacts and benefits of development and relationship to the natural environment are now couched in terms such as ecosystem services. The emergence of new fields and industry—climate finance, green jobs, and green economy—are all born from the evolving nature of green and sustainable development practice.

Green and sustainable development is not static. As knowledge of areas increases and practices implemented and refined, so too will the responses adopted in urban areas. This tool kit provides a basis for ADB staff and consultants to develop an understanding of key elements of what makes a "green city" and how development may be improved to deliver more green and sustainable outcomes.

1. Introduction

1.1 What is the Green City Development Tool Kit?

This is a reference guide (herein called the tool kit) for Asian Development Bank (ADB) staff and consultants as well as city leaders. This tool kit introduces the key concepts of Green City development and includes a summary of each sector, highlighting crosscutting themes and benefits of actions. Following the introduction of key concepts and issues, the tool kit sets out a framework for undertaking assessments of urban areas and determining green and sustainable development responses. It also provides an inventory of current and existing resources that complement and support the design and preparation of green and sustainable development actions.

1.2 Why is the Tool Kit Needed?

Asia is urbanizing rapidly. It is predicted that from 2015, population growth in Asia will predominantly occur in urban centers.[2] Pressure on resources and increased demand on local and global environments, coupled with the need and expectation to improve the overall quality of life of residents, means that the decisions taken by governments (across all levels) and its populace have never been more important. The concept of "Green City" or "Green Development" is not new. Previously couched within the term "sustainable development," it seeks to integrate environmental, social, and economic considerations within development processes. A Green City or Green Development is an extension of this concept but is understood within the frame of a city's actions and how these actions contribute to a city or urban area advancing as green and sustainable. Green Development considers how to improve and manage the overall quality and health of water, air, and land in urban spaces; its correlation with hinterlands and wider systems; and the resultant benefits derived by both the environment and residents.

In Asia, Green Cities or Green Development is essential. Most urban cities in Asia are struggling to meet their infrastructure needs; maintain or provide adequate service delivery; and upgrade city systems to keep pace with the rate of change, urbanization, and population gain. In addition, limitations in human and financial capital, technical expertise, and low community awareness all contribute to the challenge for city leaders and government to implement urban upgrading and development initiatives. Compounding these challenges, scarce natural resources and depleted or degraded natural environments within and around urban areas often means that the required improvement and investments are starting at a low baseline, increasing the potential up-front costs and often requiring significant justification to gain the necessary support to proceed. Similarly, increased vulnerability—as a result of climate change and exposure to disaster events—shapes the development needs of urban areas and places pressure on scarce resources. Further, inappropriate land use location, poor governance, and weak legislation and enforcement capacity exacerbate urban and city centers' inability to "go green."

ADB's Urban Operational Plan 2012–2020 encapsulates the sustainable development concept within three initiatives, known as the 3E approach. The 3E approach frames city development within the context of *economy* (the competitive city), *equity* (the inclusive city), and *environment* (the Green City). Each initiative sets out the key components for achieving such a city and supports the other, providing the basis for sustainable urban development.

---

[2]   M. Lindfield and F. Steinberg, eds. 2012. *Green Cities*. Manila: Asian Development Bank.

The Green City and promotion of green development recognize that cities are dynamic, have limited resources, need resilient infrastructure (hard and soft), and are able to deliver the quality of life benefits expected by its residents. Cities can also provide greater opportunity for the private sector to engage and deliver green development outcomes. This tool kit is therefore situated within this context and has been prepared as a means of sign posting ADB staff and consultants, and partners; decision makers; and civil society groups to a range of resources that can assist in developing, progressing, and enhancing the green city agenda. Importantly, the tool kit recognizes that the development of a city is iterative, that cities are dynamic, and that no two cities are the same. Accordingly, this variation and dynamism provides the potential for innovative responses to be developed and incremental change to occur.

The transition of cities through the development curve can correspond, but not always, with that of the transition to different stages of a "green city." As resources and capacity permit, the investments taken in cities influence how quickly and effectively this transition takes place. However, this correlation is not always neat. The economic status of a city does not always translate into higher investment or achievement of green development.

Central to the success of green development and city development is increased knowledge and participation of residents and the community. Early engagement with the community to identify needs, to promote understanding and awareness of key issues, and to obtain inputs into design processes provides invaluable local context and knowledge, and supports the development of community-led responses. Community engagement supports knowledge transfer and education initiatives—an important element and basis for long-term sustainability.

Situating green development within the context of livability and improved urban environments enables a more practical understanding of the importance of green development initiatives and its relationship to individuals. Developing indicators that can assist city leaders and community track progress that relates to the livability of cities is a useful tool to improve knowledge and encourage accountability as well as celebrating success. Tracking progress and transition through the development and green city cycle is therefore important, and the tool kit also provides an introduction and/or framework for establishing indicators leading, ultimately, to the establishment of an index.

1.3   How is the Tool Kit Structured?

The guide is structured in four main sections (Figure 1.1).

This tool kit complements the five stages of the ADB project cycle and can be applied in various forms at each stage. For ease of use, this tool kit has streamlined the project or program cycle into three steps:

Implementation has not been captured specifically as the emphasis of this tool kit is on introducing key concepts to enable the development and design of appropriate interventions vis-à-vis guidance on *how to* implement such projects. Thus, the tool kit introduces key concepts to users and explains interrelationships across urban sectors and themes while highlighting currently available resources that will help identify key issues, design appropriate green city interventions, and identify the tools available to evaluate progress.

Figure 1.1: Tool Kit Structure

Section 1: Introduction	• Introduction to tool kit • Context—Why is green city development important? • Outline of tool kit contents
Section 2: Green Cities and their Components	• Defining green cities • Integrated urban development • Green city investments
Section 3: The Three-Step Approach	• Preparing a city profile and needs assessment • Plugging the gaps—Identifying additional assessment and analysis requirements • Identifying priorities and programming investment • Design and evaluation
Section 4: Inventory of Available Resources	• Sector and theme-based analytical tools • Further reading • Identification of crosscutting themes

Figure 1.2: Three-Step Approach

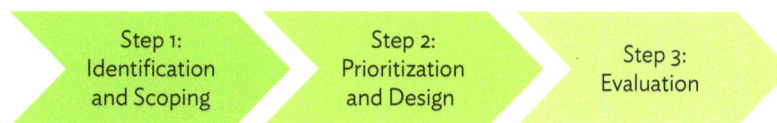

Step 1: Identification and Scoping → Step 2: Prioritization and Design → Step 3: Evaluation

Source: Emma Lewis adapted from ADB guidance http://www.adb.org/projects/cycle

Figure 1.3: The ADB Project Cycle and the Tool Kit

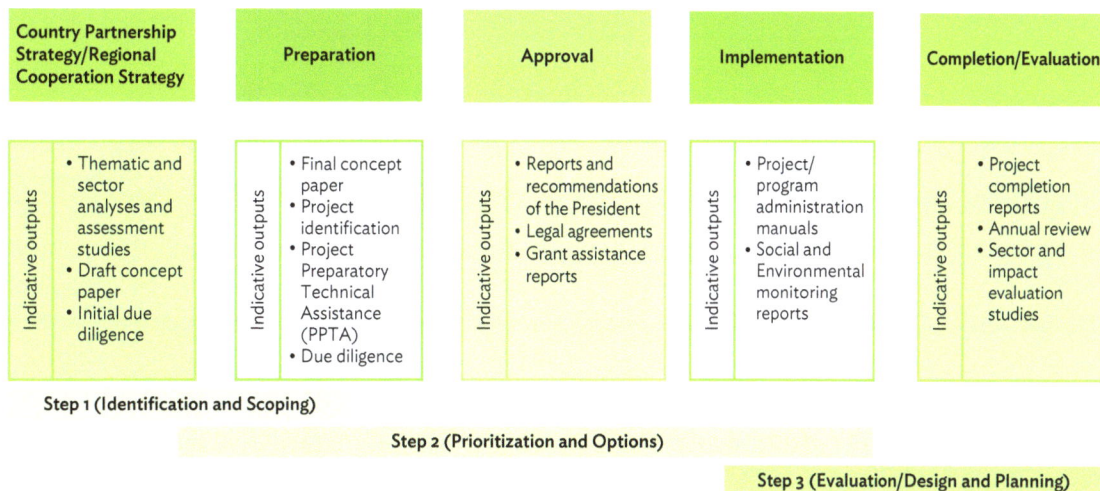

Country Partnership Strategy/Regional Cooperation Strategy	Preparation	Approval	Implementation	Completion/Evaluation
Indicative outputs: • Thematic and sector analyses and assessment studies • Draft concept paper • Initial due diligence	Indicative outputs: • Final concept paper • Project identification • Project Preparatory Technical Assistance (PPTA) • Due diligence	Indicative outputs: • Reports and recommendations of the President • Legal agreements • Grant assistance reports	Indicative outputs: • Project/program administration manuals • Social and Environmental monitoring reports	Indicative outputs: • Project completion reports • Annual review reports • Sector and impact evaluation studies

Step 1 (Identification and Scoping)

Step 2 (Prioritization and Options)

Step 3 (Evaluation/Design and Planning)

Source: Emma Lewis adapted from ADB guidance http://www.adb.org/projects/cycle

2. Green Cities and Their Components

Green Cities minimize environmental impact and maximize opportunities to improve and support the natural environment. Green Cities are energy efficient and reduce reliance on nonrenewable energy sources; actively encourage waste reduction and management; include green and resilient infrastructure, low-carbon transport, and water cycle management; and deliver improved quality of life outcomes for residents.

Cities are dynamic, and complex. Asia is urbanizing rapidly, increasing pressure on resources and infrastructure, and simultaneously influencing the living conditions and quality of life conditions for inhabitants. How Asian cities respond to these challenges has local, regional, and international reach. *Green City* does not have a universal definition and therefore will mean many different things to different people. Along the same lines, there is no universal solution that can be applied to every city in any country. Adaptable, responsive, and innovative solutions that differ from one place to another enable Green Cities to emerge in various guises and recognize the variation and dynamism of cities.

Providing a definition of Green Cities needs to be situated within this dynamic context and provide a framework for how key themes can be implemented, adapted, and developed at the city level. The United Nations' Agenda 21 initiative of the early 1990s began to mainstream sustainable development principles within planning and development processes. Since then, knowledge and practice have continued to develop. Green Cities can be considered the contemporary name for which areas develop in a manner that is socially responsible, and environmentally and economically sustainable, as captured by ADB in its 3E approach.

Although there is no uniform definition of "Green City," several central themes help shape and define what a Green City is. Such themes include energy efficiency (including built form) and reducing reliance on nonrenewable energy sources, sustainable and low-carbon transportation systems, green and resilient infrastructure, waste reduction and management, increased green areas, water cycle management, and integrated planning. How a city develops as green varies across geography, sector, and pace at which it occurs. Decisions taken by city leaders on where, what, and how investment will be directed to support green development need to be considered when adopting a system-based approach. A system-based approach recognizes the interconnectedness of sectors and the importance of sequencing.[3] It also recognizes that cities will evolve to different levels of "green" at different rates and that this development is not uniform.

Figure 2.1 provides a conceptual framework of how cities transition to various levels of "green," commencing at basic and progressing to eco and then carbon positive.[4] This framework provides a basis for cities to operate and track progress within. The framework is not rigid, and some cities may find their experience and development spread across multiple categories, that is, one sector may be eco, another basic, and another carbon positive. Such variation is not uncommon and highlights the importance of being able to perceive the "bigger" picture of cities and the relationship between sectors. Similarly, the framework highlights one of the great opportunities for Asian

---

[3]   Sequencing refers to development in a staged and coordinated manner. It identifies the "sequence" or the order in which development should take place. Such an approach assumes that certain basic or foundational elements need to be in place before other aspects of development can take place. It can help cities prioritize investment and help minimize future retrofitting.

[4]   The categorization and aim for "carbon positive" is not intended in this instance as an absolute. It is, in abroad sense, a vision or objective that a city can aim to achieve but is integrated across many other initiatives. It supposes that cities that have transitioned to a more "advanced" state will be using the full range of instruments to minimize environmental impact and enhance the green and sustainable nature of their city.

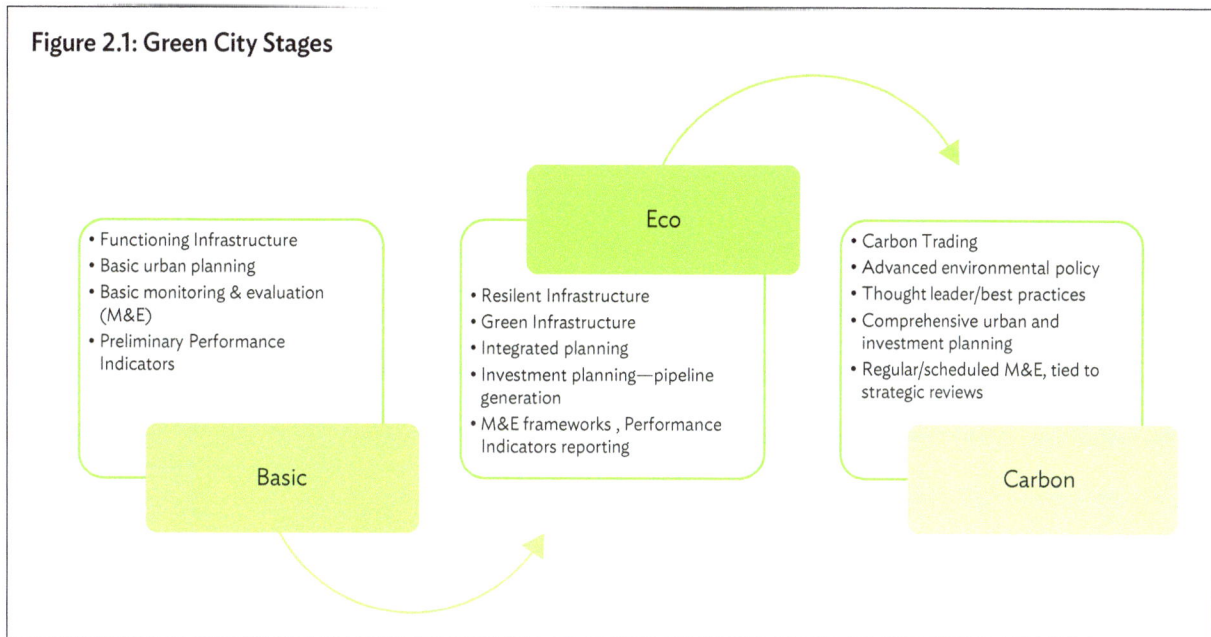

Figure 2.1: Green City Stages

- Functioning Infrastructure
- Basic urban planning
- Basic monitoring & evaluation (M&E)
- Preliminary Performance Indicators

Basic

Eco

- Resilent Infrastructure
- Green Infrastructure
- Integrated planning
- Investment planning—pipeline generation
- M&E frameworks , Performance Indicators reporting

- Carbon Trading
- Advanced environmental policy
- Thought leader/best practices
- Comprehensive urban and investment planning
- Regular/scheduled M&E, tied to strategic reviews

Carbon

cities and that is an increased entry point for some sectors. The benefit of lessons learned from the industrialization period and subsequent technological advances means that cities may be able to skip a step and potentially avoid the negative impacts of development associated with older or poorer practices. The framework also provides the basis for developing and implementing monitoring and evaluation mechanisms (including indicators) that enable progress to be tracked and adjustments to planning and investment to be made.

The correlation between economic status and attainment of the various tiers of a green city is not always neat. Just as different sectors will be at different stages of development within the green city cycle, so too is the variation between economic status and investment in green development. Factors that influence this include financial resources, institutional and technical capacity, awareness of issues, and competing interests within government. While it may hold true that low-income countries are more likely to be at "basic," it is also likely that middle-income countries will have aspects of city development at this stage. High-income countries are not precluded from being at "basic" either. However, it is probable that how cities transition from basic to carbon positive is influenced most by economic capacity and increased awareness of issues.

Relating transition within a green city framework (Figure 2.2) highlights two things. First, as gross domestic product (GDP) increases and the transition from low- to high-income country occurs, so does the adoption of green planning and technologies. The second involves reflecting the stages of green city development. Combining these elements in one figure is a useful way of relating economic growth (expressed via country income levels) and that of transition toward green city objectives at a sector investment level and relationship to urban planning. Considering green development in this manner recognizes that the types of investment choices will change over time and continue to change as a city moves through the various "levels" of city planning and development toward green city.

A recent research study conducted by the International Council for Local Environmental Initiatives (ICLEI–Local Governments for Sustainability) and the London School of Economics (LSE)[5] has begun to examine what they

---

[5]   *Going Green: How Cities are Leading the Next Economy.* A global survey of city governments on the green economy. The Rio+20 Edition. 2012.

Figure 2.2: Green City Progression

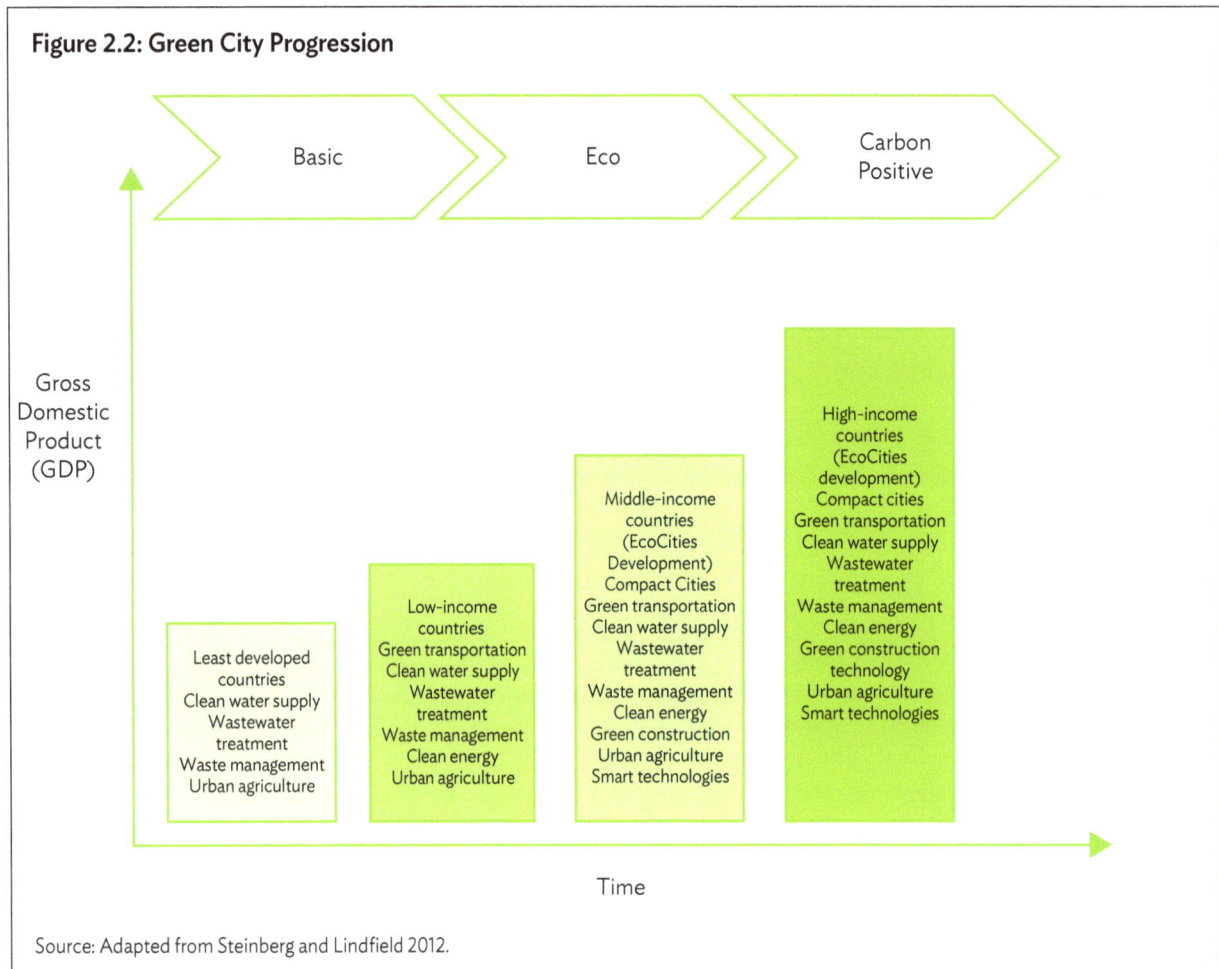

Basic → Eco → Carbon Positive

Gross Domestic Product (GDP)

Least developed countries
Clean water supply
Wastewater treatment
Waste management
Urban agriculture

Low-income countries
Green transportation
Clean water supply
Wastewater treatment
Waste management
Clean energy
Urban agriculture

Middle-income countries (EcoCities Development)
Compact Cities
Green transportation
Clean water supply
Wastewater treatment
Waste management
Clean energy
Green construction
Urban agriculture
Smart technologies

High-income countries (EcoCities development)
Compact cities
Green transportation
Clean water supply
Wastewater treatment
Waste management
Clean energy
Green construction technology
Urban agriculture
Smart technologies

Time

Source: Adapted from Steinberg and Lindfield 2012.

referred to as key triggers or prompts for city governments "to go green." The study ranked responses to the following: How important are the following triggers in making green objectives as important parts of your city's political agenda? Six triggers were outlined and included (and ranked in order of response priority):

• Public opinion/awareness
• A change in local leadership
• Pressure from national/supranational government
• Sewage treatment and disposal
• A particular crisis (not related to environment)
• Others

These findings highlight the importance of community participation within green city development and moreover how it can be leveraged to encourage change. Community participation and early engagement[6] are central to the success of green and sustainable development initiatives and transition through development stages. The

---

[6]   Two useful online references that provide a succinct and practical summary of approaches can be accessed here:
http://www.communityplanningtoolkit.org/sites/default/files/Engagement.pdf
http://www.qld.gov.au/web/community-engagement/guides-factsheets/documents/engaging-queenslanders-methods-and-techniques.pdf

full breadth of engagement techniques needs to be employed (information–consultation–participation) and complemented with sustained support.

Cities are not homogeneous and as such even within cities different responses will be required. What is important is that cities can situate their position within a greater context and that there is a "feedback" loop that enables the iterative process of planning and development to be reflected in strategies, projects, and programs as they take place.

Adopting a Green City approach to development in Asian cities encourages development of urban spaces that can deliver benefits to both residents and the natural environment. According to Lehmann (2009), ultimately, the aim for cities adopting a Green City approach is that, through integrated planning and investments, urban environments will

- respond well to their climate, location, orientation, and context, optimizing natural assets such as sunlight and wind flow;
- are quiet(er), clean, and effective, with a healthy microclimate;
- have reduced or have no carbon dioxide emissions, as they are self-sufficient energy producers, powered by renewable energy sources; and
- eliminate the concept of waste, as they are based on a closed-loop ecosystem with significant recycling, reusing, remanufacturing, and composting.

(Lehmann 2009)

The following section sets out the key elements to help define Green Cities. It introduces important basic concepts that need to be reflected in green city strategies, projects, and programs.

2.1   Urban Resilience

Urban Resilience is an overarching and important concept that must be considered as part of Green Cities. The term is used to describe the capacity of cities to respond, adapt, function, and evolve to a changing climate and related shocks and stresses and disaster events. Importantly, it considers both the built form and human elements of a city and more specifically, the ability of people living and working—particularly the poor and vulnerable—to survive and recover.

Urban resilience considers climate change adaptation, mitigation actions, and disaster risk reduction initiatives within the complexity of urban systems and the uncertainty related to climate change. This means that building resilience is founded on the importance of understanding *how* a city functions, the boundaries of control and influence of different actors within the city, and how the city as a whole can evolve and adapt so that urban populations and especially the urban poor can survive when faced with a wide range of volatile shocks or stresses (ADB 2014).

For a concise and instructive reference guide for urban resilience, refer to the ADB publication *Urban Climate Change Resilience: A Synopsis*.

2.2   Integrated Urban Development

Integrated Urban Development is a term used to describe the consideration of multiple sectors and objectives within a planning and development process and often, needing to reconcile conflicting development objectives. Integrated urban development is relevant to Green Cities as it enables the planning and development process to consider how an urban area will develop with green and sustainable principles in mind and with regard to how the interplay between sectors helps to achieve such outcomes.

ADB, through its Urban Operational Plan (UOP), will support its developing member countries (DMCs) in developing their urban economies, improving environmental sustainability, and in making pro-poor investments. This provides an opportunity for the **urban sector** to play an integrating role, and an avenue to focus ADB's operations, beyond traditional urban investment sectors in order to maximize their impact (ADB 2011a).

UOP 2012 sets out a new direction and an approach for ADB urban sector operations to proactively respond to current and anticipated future needs by effectively addressing the investment opportunities and programmatic issues hindering the efficient, sustainable, and equitable development of cities. To enable an integrative process to maximize the impact of urban sector investments, ADB's UOP promotes the 3E approach comprising the three dimensions of Sustainability—Economy (competitive), Environment (green), and Equity (inclusive)—and a tool kit for each prepared, with Green City the subject of this tool kit. Collectively, these tool kits provide practical guidance and information to support the growth and development of cities in line with the 3E approach.

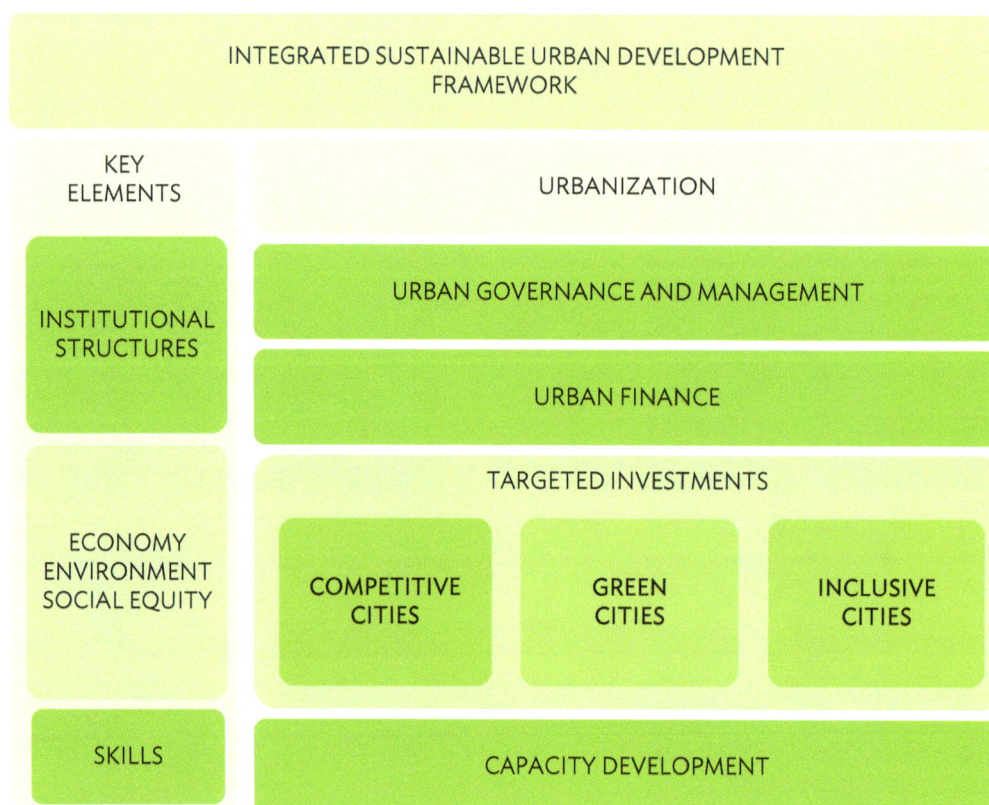

Figure 2.3: Integrated Sustainable Urban Development Framework

Source: Asian Development Bank.

Developing an Integrated Approach for Green Development

Developing an integrated approach for Green Development need not be complicated. While at times the volume and breadth of issues for consideration seem vast, integrated green development is iterative; responsive; and developed over short-, medium-, and long-term time horizons. Each city will have different entry points based on the urban environment, financial resources, and institutional capacity. Integrated green development is a conceptual framework and an understanding of how elements "fits together" within the overarching goal to achieve "green principles" as outlined above.

Developing an integrated green development approach requires several key components to be in place or worked toward putting in place. These are

- **Policy and Regulatory Framework**: Each sector should be supported by an enabling regulatory and policy framework that is consistent with a city's ambition and vision of being green. Appropriate regulatory control that is cascaded into policy documents and advice for government officials and departments to follow.
- **Strategic Planning**: This is the process of visioning (including community and stakeholder engagement) and setting the long-term development objective(s) for an urban area. This includes what avenues a city can pursue to achieve green and sustainable development outcomes and what infrastructure/services are required to support this vision/objective and residents. Strategic planning provides a development vision that is related and connected to budgetary, performance, and monitoring and evaluation systems.
- **Link to Finance**: Finances should be allocated for sectors and projects related to Green Urban Development. Apart from conventional finance, green financing mechanisms, such as Clean Development Mechanism, Global Environment Facility, Climate Investment Funds, etc., can be used. Identifying finance options also requires an assessment of current budget constraints. This will inform investment decision and choices and prioritization (see next section).

The above components provide an enabling environment and needs to be further supported by actions that include

- **Prioritization of Sectors**: Identification of those sectors and related interventions ranked in order of priority that are required to support a city becoming or developing as a Green City. Prioritization may be influenced by the level of impact a proposed intervention may have and the ability to advance/transition through the stages of a "green city." It may also be influenced by the level of current and future risks a city may face. This process will support the preparation of a project pipeline.
- **Project Development**: Specific projects selected from a project pipeline, demonstrate a multisector approach, and can be situated within the "green city stages" conceptual framework are identified and detailed out for their implementation.

As outlined in Figure 2.1 and Figure 2.2, the transitionary nature of Asian cities means that green city programs and projects need to identify and respond to existing constraints while at the same time develop with advancement in mind.

Integrated land use planning is central to contemporary planning practice and represents the critical first step whereby appropriate land use policy is derived and then translated into development frameworks and measures of development control. Contemporary planning practice requires strategic planning to be an integral element of the planning process. Through forward planning and understanding the current situation and risks of urban areas, strategic planning enables decision makers to prepare high-level plans that set a development framework and integrates considerations such as land supply and management—including climate change, natural hazards, infrastructure requirements and location (hard and soft), and open space and areas for future development expansion.

Preparing appropriate development plans is based on the acknowledgment that land use planning provides a policy mechanism that enables diverse and often conflicting objectives to be integrated and addressed in a development or spatial framework which

- identifies appropriate area(s)/location(s) for specific land uses;
- determines what current and future risks are associated with specific land uses in specific locations;
- determines and identifies sensitive or important environmental and/or societal features; and
- details minimum requirements/expectations of particular land use types.

Put simply, it determines what development is required and where it should go.

In Asia, many cities do not yet have a fully functioning land use planning and land administration system. Often, developments are undertaken in isolation and are not integrated within a wider development or investment planning framework.

It is therefore important to consider within program/project design how a feedback loop can be incorporated to enable cities to track progress through the basic-eco-carbon positive framework. Such an approach, linked to investment planning (see following section) enables a project pipeline to be developed and implemented, and thus enables city leaders to track progress and progression of green cities.

Section 2.4 of this tool kit provides an introduction to each sector and key concepts and concludes with Figure 2.7, which conceptualizes integrated urban development and draws together the features identified earlier.

2.3   Components of Green Urban Development

Identifying what investment is required in urban areas to enable economic activity, and create livable and vibrant cities in an environmentally sustainable way is the key challenge for decision makers. Identifying strategic investments and developing a project pipeline is a crucial step in city planning. Strategic Investments are those investments that have the potential to provide catalytic impacts or provide a critical enabling link to support green development within a city. More than that, strategic investments recognize the importance of sequencing to ensure maximum impact and effective delivery of services. Investment planning is the process of prioritizing actions over multiple time horizons that considers budgets and access to finance.[7] It prepares a project pipeline to ensure that actions and development are undertaken in a coordinated manner to support green and sustainable outcomes.

For green cities, six thematic investment[8] areas have been identified (see Figure 2.4). These thematic investment areas are multisectoral. The following section provides a snapshot of each of the key investment areas and identifies key considerations and benefits. It is followed by the section covering urban infrastructure sectors and which includes a summary of each of the sectors that comprise green urban development. These two sections together represent the component parts of green cities and therefore should be read in conjunction with one another.

---

[7]   See also J. Eichler, A. Wegener, and U. Zimmermann. 2012. *Financing Local Infrastructure – Linking Local Governments and Financial Markets.* Deutsche Gesellschaft für Internationale Zusammenarbeit (GIZ) GmbH.

[8]   M. Lindfield and F. Steinberg, eds. 2012. *Green Cities.* Manila: Asian Development Bank.

Figure 2.4: Components of Green City Investments

- Support to Low-Carbon Transport
- Green Industry Complex
- Energy-Efficient Buildings
- City Greening
- Green, Resilient Infrastructure
- Intelligent Systems

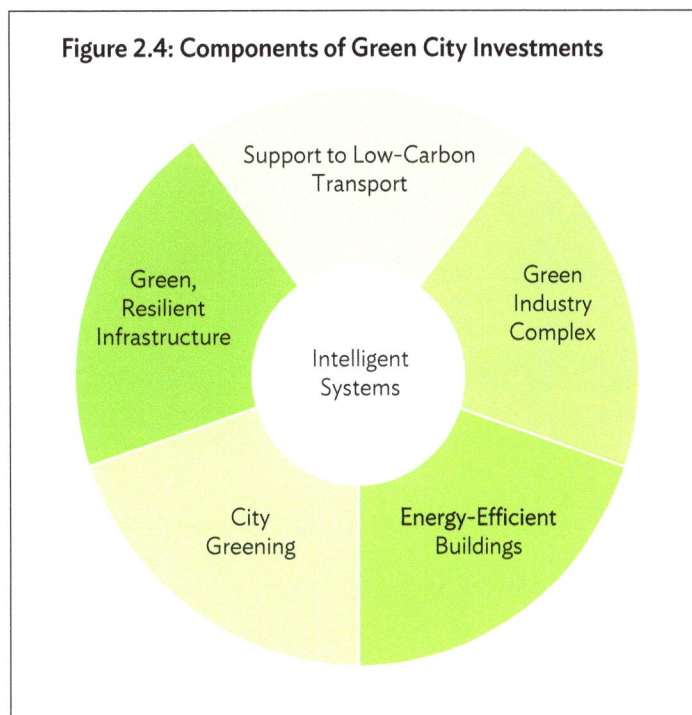

Each component is detailed in Table 2.1 through Table 2.6.

Table 2.1: Low-Carbon Transport

Summary/Snapshot

Transport systems that are accessible, safe, environment-friendly, and affordable. Asia's rapid economic development and reliance on fossil fuels/petroleum-based modes of transport has direct links to air quality and greenhouse gas (GHG) emissions, climate change, and decreased quality of life.

Low-carbon transport solutions support reducing reliance on petroleum-based modes of transport and increased emphasis and encouragement of nonmotorized and low-carbon transport.

Central to low-carbon transport solutions is Transit Oriented Development (TOD) that considers mass transit/multimodal transport hubs supported by high-density residential and mixed-use development along corridors and activity nodes/centers. Well-integrated transit and land development facilitates urban forms that reduce the need for travel by private motorized modes. Enhancing urban areas through good design that create spaces that are accessible, walkable, include city greening, green infrastructure (e.g., flood control), and serviced by efficient public transport become attractive places for people to live while simultaneously helping reduce local pollution and GHG emissions and improving living conditions.

Key Considerations	Benefits
• Integrated urban transport planning • Transit Oriented Development • Multimodal transport • Low-carbon public transport • Information technology/intelligent transport systems (ITS) • City greening and green infrastructure	• Livable cities • Reduced emissions • Reduced carbon footprint • Increased quality of life • Increased productivity through reduced commute lengths • Reduced reliance on automobiles

Table 2.2: Green Industry Complex

Summary/Snapshot

Cities with efficient recycling systems can reuse up to 75% of household waste. Manufacturing and construction generate four times as much waste as households do (Girardet 1996). The generation of industrial waste is a significant challenge in Asian economies that have strong industrial and manufacturing sectors.

Green Industry considers the multiple life cycle of various products and by-products. Put differently, the by-product on one industrial process becomes the inputs for another. Implementation of the Circle Economy (CE) approach requires both government involvement and effective institutional arrangements to enable sufficient regulatory control, coordination, and incentives for adoption of CE. Although the adoption of the CE approach includes some additional up-front costs, the economic benefits—when considered over the long term in relation to improved operating and reduced waste production and improved environment—are considered to outweigh the initial up-front expenditure.

Key Considerations	Benefits
• Government and institutional capacity/ arrangements • Involvement of producers, community groups, the industry sector • Spatial planning • Monitoring and evaluation frameworks • Training, development, and community awareness requirements	• Reduced waste output • Improved operating efficiency • Improved environmental conditions • Potential additional revenue streams • Increased awareness of waste management practices • Improved urban environmental conditions

Table 2.3: Energy-Efficient Buildings

Summary/Snapshot

Energy-efficient buildings consider both the embodied energy required to extract, process, and transport and install building materials as well as the operating energy to provide services such as heating, cooling, and powering equipment.

The design and construction of energy-efficient buildings are supported by building design standards that consider appropriate siting; solar access ; water capture, treatment, and reuse; improving operating efficiency; reducing reliance on nonrenewable energy sources; and the incorporation of alternative energy sources. Building codes ensure that minimum standards are achieved (subject to adequate enforcement). Verification and rating systems such as those issued and facilitated via green building councils and systems such as the Leadership in Energy and Environmental Design (LEED) and the Building Research Establishment Environmental Assessment Method (BREEAM) add to this by providing a marketable element to the built environment that can help promote its financial viability. Further, the various tiers of the rating and verification system provide a market-based instrument that encourages more than just doing the minimum.

Key Considerations	Benefits
• Building design standards • Rating systems • Planning and building enforcement capacity • Renewable energy • Sustainable building materials • Financial incentives • Urban planning and urban densities • City greening (green roofs, living walls, urban agriculture)	• Reduced energy and water consumption • Healthy buildings • Reduced emissions • Reduced operating costs • Less waste generation • Increased marketing potential

Table 2.4: City Greening

Summary/Snapshot

City greening considers the provision of green and open space. Linked closely also to green infrastructure, city greening considers the positive role that increased green cover has in an urban environment. More than improved visual amenity, increased green areas within the city extent help reduce the impact of heat island effect (cities absorb heat due to the level of built-up areas and, consequently, cities take longer to cool), improve air quality, improve the quality of water runoff through filtration, can function as natural buffers to natural hazards such as floods and typhoons, and increase biodiversity. City greening also provides the opportunity to increase food security in urban areas through urban farming and food production and simultaneously increasing public open space and provision of less conventional recreational areas.

Ecosystem services[9] and habitat banking or offsets are emerging fields of practice. They are more readily applied in advanced or developed economies, but that is not to say that there are elements developing countries cannot incorporate. An ecosystems approach provides a framework for looking at whole ecosystems in decision making, and for valuing the ecosystem services they provide (Defra 2011). In an urban area, considering and valuing (in economic terms) the impact of improved air or water quality has on residents provides a further policy mechanism and evaluation tool for advancing green and sustainable development.

Habitat banking or an offset system is an approach that looks to quantify the impact of a proposed development and the natural environment and provide compensatory habitat or an offset. It can be seen as a form of mitigation. In the context of Asian cities, an offset scheme provides an opportunity to incorporate greater green space within development sites but also to begin thinking at the city and landscape levels and how a green network may be developed.

Key Considerations	Benefits
• Urban farming • Heat island • Passive cooling • Green roofs • Living walls • Habitat banking/offsets • Ecosystem services • Landscape-level planning	• Improved urban environment • Improved air and water quality • Increased quality of life • Cooler urban centers • Improved visual amenity • Alternative public spaces • Increased biodiversity • Increased connection/understanding of the natural environment by residents • Reduced disaster risk

Table 2.5: Green, Resilient Infrastructure

Summary/Snapshot

Green, resilient infrastructure refers to two complementary elements of the provision of infrastructure—green and resilient. Green infrastructure has many definitions and can broadly be considered as a network of multifunctional natural and seminatural areas, features, and green spaces. Resilient infrastructure refers to the ability of infrastructure to withstand particular events such as extreme weather events (flooding) or disasters (earthquakes) and climate change.

Green infrastructure in urban areas includes addressing issues (such as drainage) that traditionally have been addressed through hard engineering solutions (capture, redirection, and discharge). Green infrastructure considers natural processes and, in the case of drainage, sustainable drainage systems to incorporate the use of permeable materials and landscaping. This response may be integrated into open space networks including walkways and bikeways. Responding to climate change and reducing vulnerability of communities are key considerations for provision of resilient infrastructure and are included within the understanding of green infrastructure. Green, resilient infrastructure considers both hard and soft engineering solutions.

Key Considerations	Benefits
• Multifunctional spaces and engineering solutions • Natural processes – systems-based approach • Short-, medium-, and long-term time horizons • Integrated urban planning • Future expansion needs • Use of technology • Building materials • Ecosystem services	• Improved service delivery • Multifunctional spaces • Adaptable and resilient urban spaces • Adaptation to climate change • Improved visual amenity • Increased biodiversity

[9] There are four main categories of ecosystem services: provisioning services, e.g., food, fiber, and fuel; regulating services, e.g., stormwater regulation, carbon sequestration; supporting services, e.g., soil formation; and cultural services, e.g., aesthetic values (Defra 2007).

Table 2.6: Intelligent Systems and Smart Cities

Summary/Snapshot
Intelligent systems refers to the use of information and communication technologies (ICTs) that helps improve the provision of data and service delivery; encourages citizen participation; and assists in making government more accountable, transparent, and effective. Such systems integrate data across numerous sectors to enable cities to operate more effectively, support decision making, and facilitate more responsive government and provision of services. The use of intelligent systems is not restricted in any urban sector and can operate at varying levels throughout each stage of a city's development as green. Intelligent systems support decision making. The convergence of technology via computer or mobile phone technology, community participation, and urban planning and management process enables data to be captured and presented spatially, enabling often geographically disbursed government officials and departments to make decisions based on locally relevant and updated information. Intelligent systems have the potential to support and improve transportation networks through real-time monitoring and control of movement flow of transport networks—including people in and around stations. Intelligent systems can also be considered within the context of disaster risk reduction and the use of early warning systems aimed at protecting communities from potentially dangerous weather events.

Key Considerations	Benefits
• Financial and institutional capacity • Technological capacity • Operation and management • Transport planning and management • Public safety and monitoring • Early warning systems (disaster risk management) • Urban service reporting	• Responsive infrastructure • Responsive government • Efficient provision of services • Resilient infrastructure • Improved disaster risk reduction • Improved transparency (government)

2.4   Urban Sectors

The tool kit covers five urban infrastructure sectors: water, solid waste, transport, energy, and buildings and built environment.

A summary of each sector identifies key issues and concepts relevant to Asian cities and focus areas for investment and value addition. These sectors form the basis for investment and preparation of performance indicators.

2.5   Water

The water sector comprises three main elements:

- Water supply
- Wastewater and sanitation
- Stormwater management and drainage

Figure 2.5 provides a summary of the urban water cycle; understanding these elements and their relationships will help establish the platform of each individual component (supply, waste, drainage) of green city development. Each component is explained in detail in the following section.

Figure 2.5: Water Cycle and Water-Sensitive Urban Design

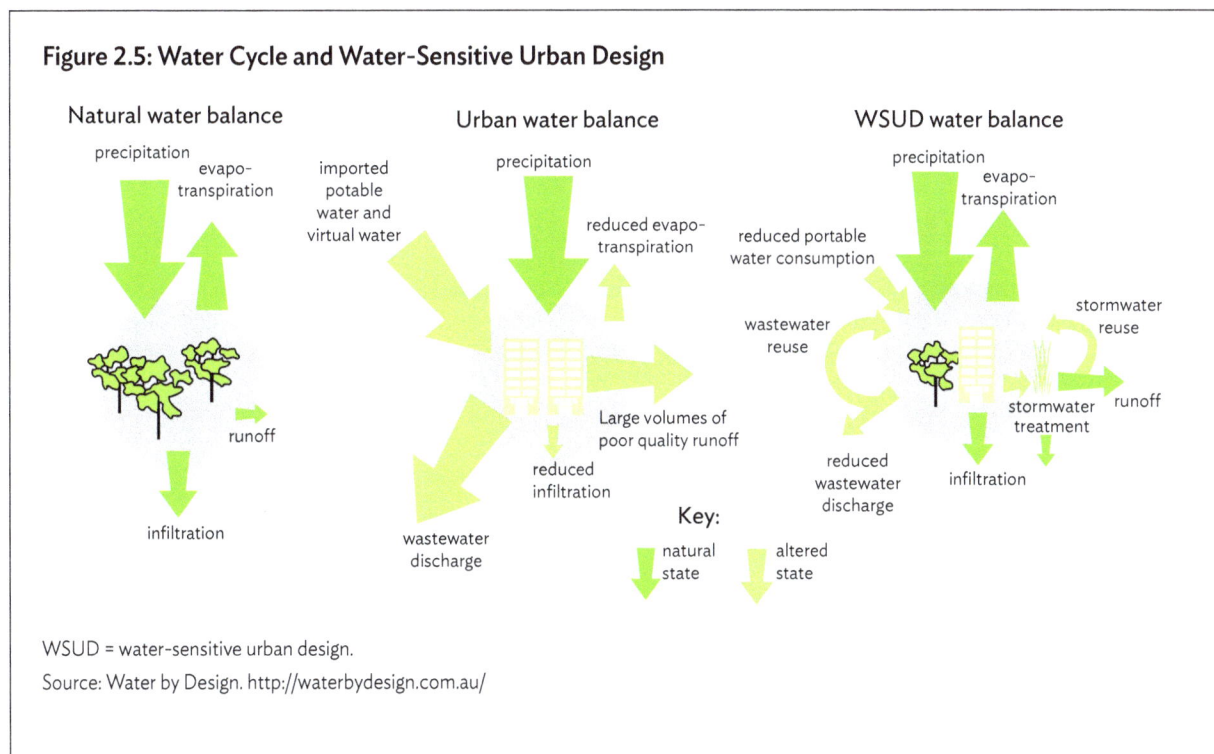

WSUD = water-sensitive urban design.

Source: Water by Design. http://waterbydesign.com.au/

Sector: Water Supply

Summary

Water supply is no longer defined as solely providing water to a defined set of users within a particular geographic area; rather, it encompasses sustainability and inclusive growth (ADB 2012). Access to safe water is one of the key requirements for safe and healthy living environment. Rapid urbanization and climate change have impacted the quality of water resources and the regularity of supply and access. Demand-side issues involve more than just the provision of potable water: with increased population comes increased demand for water especially in the agriculture and industry sectors. The allocation of water between these sectors and water suppliers' ability to provide water to users at all times are major challenges facing Asian cities. Currently, in most Asian cities, less than 30% of residents enjoy a constant, 24-hour supply of water. For the majority of residents without 24-hour water supply, water has to be sourced independently and often at a disproportionately higher cost.

Water supply cannot be considered in isolation. Stormwater management and drainage, wastewater collection, and solid waste management are integral elements of water supply. The lack of wastewater collection and treatment (often combined with poor or absent legislative provisions) has had a detrimental impact on water supply. Poor practices and the lack of enforcement of appropriate wastewater collection and treatment exacerbate the contamination of water supply which, in turn, contributes to the spread of waterborne diseases that pose health risks to users.

Integrated water resource management (IWRM) is a systems-based approach to managing water resources. It considers watershed (also termed river basin) management and how activities and demand at various points within the watershed impact the health and access to the water resource. In addition to the environmental elements of IWRM, social and economic factors,such as managing livelihoods and ensuring equitable access, are also considered.

Within an urban context, depending on the city, IWRM is likely to extend beyond city boundaries and potentially across multiple administrative areas. This highlights the importance of institutional and legislative frameworks to include provision for cross-boundary working. Development and actions taken upstream have impacts on downstream communities. Environmental degradation and the damming or redirection of water all contribute to the multitude of issues that need to be considered within an IWRM framework.

Water security is a significant challenge for cities in the 21st century. Water security refers to the ability of an area to access, retain, and maintain acceptable quantity and quality of water to support its full range of activities. Such requirements are becoming increasingly more difficult as the impacts of population gain, city growth, and environmental degradation are experienced. The five key dimensions[10] for Asian cities are household security, economic water security, urban water security, environmental water security, and resilience to water-based disasters. Together, these capture the multiplicity of water in people's lives. Water security also highlights the importance and challenge of providing water that is "fit for purpose." IWRM is an approach that considers how a city or urban area fits within a wider context (catchment area) and what factors influence water security, thus enabling appropriate planning and mitigation measures to be developed.

The central tenets of IWRM and water security are captured in the concept of a "water-sensitive city." Like the various stages of a green city, a water-sensitive city considers the various stages of city and urban development as it relates to water, starting with basic water supply through to water cycle management and achievement of integrated development approaches.

Interventions within the water supply sector will most likely occur at two main points—legislative and institutional reform and capacity building; and infrastructure provision such as trunk infrastructure/network piping and water treatment facility. Environmental management and improved land management practices are crosscutting themes that also support the provision of green, resilient infrastructure and adaptation to climate change.

The cost of water (including wastewater) services is impacted by energy use. There is a strong and direct relationship between water use and energy savings, leading to the term "watergy" (World Bank 2010). "Watergy" is the term used to describe the nexus between water and energy within municipal water systems. Watergy efficiency denotes the interconnections between water and energy savings, combining activities that conserve water with energy efficiency measures that reduce energy consumption, and synergies resulting from comanaging energy and water resource (Alliance to Save Energy 2002).

The provision of water supply infrastructure can also be considered through implementation mechanisms such as public–private partnerships (PPP) and models such as build–own–operate (BOO), build–own–operate–transfer (BOOT), and design–build–operate–maintain (DBOM).

---

[10] ADB. 2013. *Asian Water Development Outlook 2013. Measuring Water Security in Asia and the Pacific.* Manila.

Sector: Water Supply

Key Issues	Key Concepts
• Water security • Water balance • Pollution/Waste Management • Over-abstraction through licensing • Remedial actions (e.g., desilting river) • Climate change adaptation • Financial and Institutional capacity • Green infrastructure • Wastewater treatment and reuse • Revenue collection • Implementation models (PPP, BOO, BOOT, DBOM)	• Watershed management • Integrated Water Resource Management (IWRM) • Integrated Urban Water Management (IUWM) • Watergy • Modular Planning • Water-sensitive city/Water-sensitive urban design • Rainwater harvesting

Value-Added Options/Investment	
• Functional basic infrastructure • Green Infrastructure • Revenue collection	• City Greening

Available Resources	
• SWITCH: SWITCH Training Kit • Watergy • Riverlife • UNEP: Application of Sustainability Assessments of Technologies	• WSP–World Bank: Water and Sanitation for All Tool kit • WHO: Tools for Assessing the O&M of Water Supply and Sanitation in Development Countries • WSP: Guidance Notes on Services for the Urban Poor

Further Reading

- Asian Development Bank. 2013. *Asian Water Development Outlook 2013: Measuring Water Security in Asia and the Pacific.* Manila. *The publication provides a summary of water security in Asia and Pacific countries; introduces key concepts and considerations; and provides recommendations to improve, incentivize, plan, and manage resources and services.*
- R. Brown, N. Keath, and T. Wong. 2009. Urban Water Management in Cities: Historical, Current and Future Regimes. *Water Science and Technology.* 59(5). pp. 847–855. *A concise summary of various stages of water city.*
- N. Carter, R. Kreutzwiser, and R. de Loe. 2005. Closing the Circle: Linking Land Use Planning and Water Management at the Local Level. *Land Use Policy.* 22 (2). pp. 115–117. *A summary of lessons learned as related to land use planning and water management.*
- D. Grey, and C. Sadoff. 2007. Sink or Swim? Water Security for Growth and Development. *Water Policy.* 9 (6).pp. 545–571. IWA Publishing.
- M. Lindfield and F. Steinbergeds. 2012. *Green Cities.* Manila: Asian Development Bank. *A comprehensive and detailed publication on green cities.*
- D. Rodriguez, C. van de Berg, and A. McMahon. 2012. *Investing in Water Infrastructure: Capital, Operations and Maintenance.* Washington, DC: World Bank. *The paper examines major financing challenges in water infrastructure, providing examples and lessons learned;it also outlines two tools: expenditure reviews and results-based financing.*
- P. Gleick, M. Palaniappan, and M. Lang. 2008. *A Review of Decision-Making Support Tools in the Water, Sanitation, and Hygiene Sector. Each chapter provides an additional related reading list.*
- World Bank. 2010. Eco[2] Cities Book *This publication adopts a sector-based approach to explain EcoCities and relationships across sectors, and provides an annex of sector notes.*

Crosscutting Themes and Considerations	
• Solid waste management • Land use planning • Energy • Sustainable Land Management • Disaster resilience • Governance	• Municipal capacity and technical capacity • Climate Change Adaptation • Resilience • Biodiversity • Livelihoods

Sector: Wastewater and Sanitation

Summary

The definition of sanitation can be understood at two broad levels. The first, the individual level, is defined as the safe management of human excreta, which includes the provision of facilities, such as latrines, in combination with education and behavior change promoting hygienic practices (e.g., hand washing) to reduce fecal–oral diseases. The second, environmental sanitation, is a broader term that encompasses excreta disposal, solid waste management, wastewater disposal, vector control, and drainage, as well as the provision of appropriate sanitation facilities and support for behavior change. The latter definition represents an integrated urban development approach.

Environmental sanitation is necessary for the proper management of urban environments and to improve and protect human health as well as the natural environment. Those areas that lack the necessary infrastructure to collect, treat, and dispose of wastewater face numerous human and environmental health problems. Two critical elements relate to sanitation: water supply and wastewater collection (sewerage system). Water supply is required to enable necessary sanitation practices, while wastewater collection is required to enable the appropriate capture, treatment, and disposal of waste which will help prevent contamination of water sources as well as environmental degradation. In urban development projects, *if* water supply is being proposed and developed then this must be considered and implemented simultaneously with a sewerage system or means of collecting the wastewater (septic tank/septage system). Consideration must also be given for the type of facility that is to be introduced, for example, whether this system is to be centralized or to be decentralized. Population, density, topography, the natural environment, and potential cost of the investment are factors that will influence this decision.

In many Asian cities, public toilets are provided but may not have sufficient water supply, are inappropriately located, are not maintained, and/or may not be suitable for use by women (particularly during nighttime). Similarly, many households that share one toilet may face similar problems with water supply and waste collection. As a result, open defecation is still a part of many urban residents' life and disproportionately affecting the urban poor. Thus, the provision of appropriate sanitation facilities and the collection, treatment, and disposal of waste are essential components of urban development.

The impact of inadequate wastewater collection and treatment on the natural environment is stark. Discharge of untreated effluent and industrial waste has a deleterious effect on the health of watercourses and its ecosystem. Eutrophication through excessive nutrient discharge, contaminated freshwater sources, and degraded aquatic environment are all outcomes of poor wastewater and surface water management. Coupled with these challenges, inadequate drainage and preparedness for heavy rain events often means that wet season and instances of high rainfall are compounded by poor or absent solid waste management and exacerbate the challenges that cities face in managing water resources, as it impacted by through localized flooding, contamination of water resources (through effluent combined fresh water).

In many instances, wastewater and sanitation infrastructure is not a priority for Asian municipal administrations as it is not seen as revenue generating. Improving the fiscal base and capacity for wastewater collection must be considered in the context of green cities as functional and well-maintained sewerage system represents a fundamental building block of green city development.

Key Issues	Key Concepts
• Pollution/Waste Management • Land Availability • Capacity – current and future • Financial and Institutional capacity • Safety of women and girls • Increased awareness/education • Revenue collection	• Environmental sanitation • Recycling and wastewater reuse • Waste-to-energy • PPP implementation models • Centralized/Decentralized infrastructure provision • Modular planning

Value-Added Options/Investment

• Biogas digesters • Methane capture • Sludge treatment and reuse (e.g., production of fertilizer)	• Sale of treated wastewater (revenue) • Creation of green/open/recreational space (multifunctional green infrastructure) • City Greening

Available Resources

- SWITCH: SWITCH Training Kit
- World Bank: Design decision support
- WSSCC: Hygiene and Sanitation Software: An Overview of Approaches
- WSP: Guidance Notes on Services for the Urban Poor
- UNEP: Application of Sustainability Assessments of Technologies

Sector: Wastewater and Sanitation

Further Reading

- C. Lüthi, A. Morel, E. Tilley, and L. Ulrich. 2011. Community-led Environmental Sanitation Planning: CLUES. *A comprehensive guide and summary of 30 tools to support community-led sanitation planning; also includes worked examples.*
- C. Lüthi, A. Panesar, T. Schütze, A. Norström, J. McConville, J. Parkinson, D. Saywell, and R. Ingle. 2011. *Sustainable Sanitation in Cities – A Framework for Action. A summary of key issues facing decision makers and urban managers;outlines response for integrating sanitation into broader urban management practice and developing sustainable interventions;reflects a systems-based approach and identifies additional reference materials.*
- World Bank. 2010. Eco² Cities *Book. This publication adopts a sector-based approach to explain EcoCities and relationships across sectors, and provides an annex of sector notes.*
- M. Lindfield and F. Steinberg, eds. 2012. *Green Cities.* Manila: Asian Development Bank. *A comprehensive and detailed publication on green cities.*
- *A Review of Decision-Making Support Tools in the Water, Sanitation and Hygiene Sector.*
- Water Supply & Sanitation Collaborative Council. 2010. Hygiene and Sanitation Software: An Overview of Approaches. Geneva, Switzerland..

Crosscutting Themes and Considerations

- Solid Waste Management
- Climate Change Adaptation
- Sustainable Land Management
- Energy

- Resilience
- Biodiversity
- Livelihoods
- Land use planning

Sector: Stormwater and Drainage

Summary

Stormwater management and drainage is the final and most important element of the water sector. The capacity of a city to cope with rainfall, drain effectively, and maximize opportunities for stormwater collection and reuse is essential for the long-term sustainability of Asian cities. Stormwater management and drainage is multifaceted and is closely linked to flood risk management and green infrastructure. Inadequate stormwater management and drainage is most pronounced in urban areas that feature watercourses and are sited on or near floodplains or low-lying areas. Many Asian cities have these features and, as a result, many residents (often the urban poor) are most impacted during seasonal rains and heavy storm events.

Rapid urbanization, poor urban planning and building control, and institutional and financial capacity constraints of city governments have rendered many Asian cities incapable of putting in place adequate stormwater management and drainage systems. Conversion of land to urban uses through building construction and provision of infrastructure such as roads means pervious surfaces become less pervious as materials such as concrete and asphalt are used. This affects the flow of water and drainage capacity of an area. Often, drainage systems are absent and water falls and is not directed, captured, treated, and discharged appropriately. As a result, localized flooding occurs, water collection and reuse is not optimized, and the quality of water resources diminished as a result of pollution.

Similarly, in many areas, drainage systems are often poorly maintained and clogged with waste, increasing pollution and rendering the system ineffective. Stormwater management and drainage therefore needs to be considered within a system-based approach that recognizes the influence of urban drainage within the wider context of watershed management, flood control, environmental health, and wastewater treatment and reuse.

Sustainable Drainage Systems (SuDS) are a sequence of water management practices and facilities designed to drain surface water and to mimic natural drainage. Practices refer to improved land use planning and location of potentially polluting activities, water harvesting, and improved urban design and building standards. Facilities refer to the use of permeable surfaces; green infrastructure such as wetlands, filtration and infiltration systems, swales, and detention basins; and underground storage.

The SuDS management train (susdrain) is an approach that aims to maximize the benefits of SuDS and to incrementally manage pollution, flow rates, and volumes of water runoff. The SuDS management train considers the following steps:

1. Prevention: Considers site design, land use planning, and pavement and built area surfaces to reduce and manage runoff and pollution.
2. Source Control: Runoff managed as close as possible to the source—management techniques include the use of green roofs, rainwater harvesting, permeable paving, and filter strips.
3. Site Control: Runoff managed in a network across a site or local area through the use of swales, detention basins, etc. These public realm solutions also fulfill a multifunctional green infrastructure role.
4. Regional Control: Downstream management of runoff for whole site/catchment, such as retention ponds and wetlands.

Sector: Stormwater and Drainage

Key Issues	Key Concepts
• Water pollution • Waste management • Climate change adaptation • Financial and institutional capacity • Green infrastructure • Flood management • Urban greening • Urban design, building materials, and impervious surfaces	• Watershed management • Integrated Urban Water Management (IUWM) • Sustainable drainage systems (SuDS) • Making space for water • Rainwater harvesting • Gray water reuse

Value-Added Options/Investment	
• Functional drainage network • Green infrastructure • Integrated solid waste management and drainage systems	• City greening • Enforcement capacity building • Disaster risk reduction planning

Available Resources	
• SWITCH: SWITCH Training Kit • CIRIA: SusDrain • CIRIA: Planning for SuDS: Making It Happen	• CIRIA: Retrofitting to Manage Surface Water • Riverlife: Subcatchment Planning

Further Reading

- D. Balmforth, C. Digman, R. Kellagher, and D. Butler. 2006. *Designing for Exceedance in Urban Drainage – Good Practice.* London: Construction Industry Research and Information Association.
- M. Lindfield and F. Steinberg, eds. 2012. *Green Cities.* Manila: Asian Development Bank. *A comprehensive and detailed publication on green cities.*
- World Bank. 2010. Eco^2 Cities Book *This publication adopts a sector-based approach to explain EcoCities and relationships across sectors, and provides an annex of sector notes.*

Crosscutting Themes and Considerations	
• Climate Change Adaptation • Sustainable Land Management • Flood risk management • Resilience • Energy	• Biodiversity • Built environment • Livelihoods • Land use planning

2.6 Solid Waste

Sector: Solid Waste Management

Summary

Solid waste management refers to the collection, transfer, and disposal of waste. Asian cities employ a variety of waste management systems based on available technical and financial resources, and the current level of environmental awareness in the city concerned (ADB 2012c). This is consistent with a city's transition from basic to carbon positive within the green city framework. *Green City* solid waste management adopts the 3R approach (Reduce, Reuse, and Recycle), which can be further reflected in the "waste hierarchy" (Figure 2.6).

Figure 2.6: Waste Hierarchy

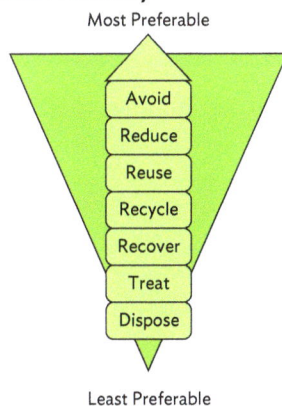

Source: Asian Development Bank.

The adoption of these principles will occur in varying degrees at all stages of city development and status within the assessment framework (basic–eco–carbon positive).

Those cities with low capacity (institutionally and financially) may employ management techniques such partial collection, open dumping, and reliance on the informal sector for collection and any reuse practices. The role of the informal sector, i.e., sorting and recovering recyclables, is often significant when cities are only able to adopt moderately low levels of solid waste management practices. As cities develop and resources allow, waste collection coverage will increase, disposal of waste via landfills, develop composting facilities, increase recovery recyclables (including mechanization) and develop and operate waste-to-energy (WTE) plants are some initiatives that can be implemented.

Poor waste management practices have negative impacts on human health and environment. Waste dumped in or near watercourses contaminate the water, restrict water flow, and lead to a degraded aquatic environment; inappropriate treatment of industrial and medical waste poses great risks to human health and the natural environment, poor practices increase vermin in urban areas, and overall poor waste management practices are a visual blight.

Forward planning that considers waste management within the context of continued urbanization and population gain also needs to consider the spatial extent of the city, the appropriate sites for waste management facilities, and the potential for cross-boundary collaboration. The ability to manage expansion and transition from lower to higher technology solutions should also be considered.

Key Issues	Key Concepts
• Open dumping • Pollution • Informal sector livelihoods • Water supply • Greenhouse gas emissions • Air quality • Land availability • Future site capacity	• 3R – reduce, reuse, recycle (waste hierarchy) • Waste-to-energy • Source point separation • Mechanization • Circle Economy (CE)

Sector: Solid Waste Management

Value-Added Options/Investment

- Waste-to-energy
- Methane capture
- Recycling facilities
- Materials recovery facility
- Transfer station
- Composting

Available Resources

- UNEP: Developing Integrated Solid Waste Management plan
- UNEP: Integrated waste management scorecard
- UNEP: Application of Sustainability Assessments of Technologies
- UNEP: Waste and Climate Change
- Tool for Rapid Assessment of City Energy
- World Bank: Social Assessment and Public Participation in Municipal Solid Waste Management

Further Reading

- M. Lindfield and F. Steinberg, eds. 2012. *Green Cities.* Manila: Asian Development Bank. *A comprehensive and detailed publication on green cities.*
- World Bank. 2010. Eco² Cities Book *This publication adopts a sector-based approach to explain EcoCities and relationships across sectors, and provides an annex of sector notes.*

Crosscutting Themes and Considerations

- Climate Change Adaptation
- Sustainable Land Management
- Resilience
- Biodiversity
- Livelihoods
- Land use planning

2.7   Transport

Sector: Transport

Summary

Arguably, no other sector attracts more amount of residents' attention than transport; everyone is affected in some way or another. Ailing or absent transport infrastructure makes daily activities in cities time-consuming, inefficient, and frustrating—negatively impacting productivity and human health. The advent of motorized transport and increased personal wealth has seen many cities grind to a halt on account of inadequate investment and provision of transport services.

ADB's sustainable transport policy is based on three elements: **Avoid–Shift–Improve**. Broadly, this strategy seeks to minimize unnecessary trips, encourage behavior change, and improve the operational efficiency of motorized transport. Or put differently:

- Land use and travel demand: interventions that influence travel behavior
- Infrastructure and services: interventions that enhance the supply or capacity of infrastructure and services
- Vehicle fleet and fuel supply: interventions that alter the number, composition, technologies, or use of vehicles and fuels

Underpinning sustainable transport is the concept of Transit Oriented Development (TOD). TOD considers the provision of mass transit systems that are supported by high residential density and mixed-use development along corridors and activity nodes and/or centers. It also considers behavior change and the nature and regularity of trips made. These considerations are captured within **Six D's**—*Destinations, Distance, Design, Density, Diversity, Demand Management.*

Policies for "Avoid"

Initiatives that can be employed to facilitate and "avoid" travel in the city include

- Zoning regulations and mixed land use planning – Alteration in existing zoning regulation to promote mixed-use development, TOD, high residential densities, and adequate provision of urban services (including employment and recreational activities) to reduce distance between workplace and living neighborhoods. Development control measures, such as floor area ratio (FAR) and floor space index (FSI), consider the amount of built form (building) in relation to the size of the development site. It provides a mechanism to influence built area to open space ratio.
- Parking control, management, and charge rates
- Road user charging (tolls, congestion charges)
- Car ownership quotas
- Car-free city areas and traffic restrictions, policy reforms are required to promote walkability.
- Demarcation of car-free zones and enforcement of traffic restrictions within the city limits can help decongest dense city core.
- Promotion of information and communication technology can be a substitute for physical travel.

Sector: Transport

Policies for "Shift"

- Develop integrated local public transport authorities
- Marketing and coordinated information provision
- Priority allocation to road space for public transport and nonmotorized transport
- Workplace / school travel plans—a walking school bus is one example of a successful school initiative to encourage walking to and from school.

Policies for "Improve"

- Low-emission zones
- Promotion of eco-driving
- Promotion of low-carbon fuels and vehicles using alternative fuels such as biofuel, biomethane, natural gas, hydrogen, or electricity.
- Standards and taxes on fuels and vehicles
- Intelligent transport systems and signaling systems

In addition, improving or upgrading existing transport systems—through provision of better facilities and services and encouraging multimodal transport hubs—offers several options for increased transport sustainability.

Ultimately, Green Cities will look to minimize reliance on personal motorized modes of transport and become a "car-lite" city, support low-carbon public transport, and have an overarching objective of becoming a zero-emission city.

Key Issues	Key Concepts
<ul><li>Congestion</li><li>Air quality and emissions</li><li>Environmental degradation</li><li>Productivity</li><li>Mass transit</li><li>Access to land</li><li>Development concessions</li><li>Affordability</li></ul>	<ul><li>Avoid – Shift – Improve</li><li>TOD</li><li>Integrated Planning</li><li>Mixed-use development</li><li>Nonmotorized transport</li><li>Six D's (Destinations, Distance, Design, Density, Diversity, Demand Management)</li><li>Energy efficiency and alternative fuels</li><li>Intelligent transport systems and Smart Cities</li></ul>
Value-Added Options/Investment	
<ul><li>Low-carbon transport</li><li>Nonmotorized transport</li><li>Integrated open space and transport planning (walkway, bikeway)</li><li>Vehicle and fuel transition/technology</li></ul>	<ul><li>Mass transit</li><li>Energy efficiency</li><li>Information and communication technology</li></ul>
Available Resources	
<ul><li>Clean Air Asia: Transport Emissions Evaluation Models for Projects</li><li>Clean Air Asia: Rapid Assessment of City Emissions</li><li>Tool for Rapid Assessment of City Energy</li></ul>	<ul><li>Clean Air Portal</li><li>UNEP: Application of Sustainability Assessments of Technologies</li></ul>
Further Reading	
<ul><li>M. Lindfield and F. Steinberg, eds. 2012. *Green Cities*. Manila: Asian Development Bank. *A comprehensive and detailed publication on green cities.*</li><li>World Bank. 2010. Eco² Cities Book *This publication adopts a sector-based approach to explain EcoCities and relationships across sectors, and provides an annex of sector notes.*</li><li>Asian Development Bank. 2010. *Sustainable Transport Initiative Operational Plan*. Manila. *A summary of ADB approach and key transport issues facing Asian cities.*</li></ul>	
Crosscutting Themes and Considerations	
<ul><li>Climate Change Mitigation and Adaptation (greenhouse gas emission planning)</li><li>Sustainable Land Management</li><li>Resilience</li></ul>	<ul><li>Biodiversity</li><li>Livelihoods</li><li>Land use planning (mixed-use development, multimodal transport hubs, urban density, network planning)</li></ul>

2.8   Energy

Sector: Energy

Summary

In rapidly urbanizing Asian cities, the energy sector is crucial. Energy is a crosscutting issue that affects transportation, built infrastructure, water supply, and solid waste management. Developing an *Energy Profile* of a city enables the level of use, mix of energy types, and patterns of use by sector or end use activity to be considered. These components are determined by a range of factors such as population, income, economic structure, energy prices, urban form, built environment, climate conditions, and access to markets (i.e., where the energy is sourced from). Developing a profile and understanding these composite parts are the initial steps of sustainable urban energy planning.

The main components for consideration in the energy sector include access, security, reliability, and affordability. Along with these components, Green Cities also consider alternative energy sources, low-carbon options, and energy efficiency. These factors are considered across multiple sectors: buildings and the built environment, transport, as well as in the sectors of industry and trade. In urban areas, buildings and transport are the two main sectors for consideration of energy-efficient development.

Improving energy efficiency is an essential element of Green Cities. Energy efficiency considers how the adoption of improved technologies and practices can contribute to reducing the energy required to provide a particular service and how this compares with energy use that does not employ such technology or practices.

Climate change and its relationship to energy production and consumption is a key consideration for green city development. Developing urban forms (spatial and built) that actively reduce consumption requirements through better design and orientation and use of alternative energy supplies is central to green city development.

Greenhouse gas (GHG) emissions linked to energy production and consumption is a major consideration for cities and climate change. The Intergovernmental Panel on Climate Change (IPCC), which was established by the United Nations Environment Programme and the World Meteorological Organization in 1998, is the leading international body fort he assessment of climate change. The IPCC publishes global assessment reports summarizing the global state and trends of climate change. It also prepares technical guidance and methodologies for undertaking assessments related to climate change.

GHG inventories are one of the major tools for calculating GHG emissions within a city and for determining the sources of GHG emissions. A GHG inventory forms the basis for preparing a GHG management framework. GHG inventories are most commonly prepared at the national level. However, emerging methodologies and practices to prepare inventories at the city level are being developed and refined. Capacity of local and municipal governments to collect, manage, and analyze data is a major constraint for many Asian cities.

Key Issues	Key Concepts
• Security of supply • Price and affordability • Alternative energy sources • Emissions and air quality • Public health • Climate change mitigation • Low carbon	• Energy Efficiency • Renewable energy • Retrofitting • Performance-based financial incentives • Lifecycle of materials • International trading schemes • GHG inventory • Cogeneration (combined heat and power)

Value-Added Options/Investment	
• Alternative energy sources: solar, wind, biofuel • Waste–to–energy	• Cobenefits—carbon trading • Combined heat and power plants • Retrofitting

Sector: Energy

Available Resources

- ICLEI: Sustainable Energy Handbook
- REEEP
- UNEP: Application of Sustainability Assessments of Technologies

- Energy Efficiency Guide for Industry in Asia
- Energy Forecasting Framework and Emissions Consensus Tool
- MACTool
- Tool for Rapid Assessment of City Energy

Further Reading

- M. Lindfield and F. Steinberg, eds. 2012. *Green Cities*. Manila: Asian Development Bank. *Comprehensive and detailed publication on green cities.*
- World Bank. 2010. Eco² Cities Book. *This publication adopts a sector-based approach to explain EcoCities and relationships across sectors, and provides an annex of sector notes.*
- Intergovernmental Panel on Climate Change. 2006. *2006 IPCC Guidelines for National Greenhouse Gas Inventories.*
- Intergovernmental Panel on Climate Change. 2003. *Good Practice Guidance for Land Use, Land-use Change and Forestry.*

Crosscutting Themes and Considerations

- Climate Change Adaptation
- Sustainable Land Management
- Resilience
- Agriculture and Food (alternative energy)

- Biodiversity
- Livelihoods
- Land use planning

2.9   Buildings and the Built Environment

Sector: Buildings and the Built Environment

Summary

The built environment can be an all-encompassing element of urban development. In the context of this tool kit and considering green cities, the built environment captures how buildings and supporting infrastructure can support a city become more green and sustainable. It considers all stages: design, construction, operation, and maintenance.

Key to the built improvement and green city is the relationship/interaction of an area's spatial extent, built form including methods and materials, transport planning, and infrastructure provision. City structure and form greatly influence energy consumption, transport modes, and overall quality of life. Urban form also influences residents' access to employment opportunities and livelihood choices (including the informal sector) based on proximity of other land uses, services, markets, and prevailing environmental conditions. Urban densities, land use planning (risk based), open space (network) planning, transport planning, and provision of service infrastructure (integrated land use planning) impact how green and sustainable principles are achieved and require control at two levels. At the macro level or city level, there must be consideration to supply, demand and capacity as well as how all the composite parts of city interact (or don't) with one another and at the site level whereby more detailed guidance is required.

At an individual site or building level, orientation; disaster risk; water capture, treatment, and reuse; energy efficiency targets and use of renewable energy; incorporation of green roofs; living walls and provision of green space (including connection to wider network); proximity to public transport; and strengthening connectivity via walkways and bikeway or secondary public transport links must all be considered. Such requirements are generally supported via planning and building ordinances or similar statutes and regulations. At the macrolevel strategic planning, which considers where development is sited based on risk exposure and vulnerability, access to transport infrastructure and the provision of basic urban services, as well as economic activity and open space, provide the overarching framework that will influence energy demand, GHG emissions, congestion, and, more broadly, the quality of the urban environment.

Green City Development Tool Kit

Sector: Buildings and the Built Environment

Intrinsically linked to green cities are resilient buildings, particularly those located along coastlines, floodplains, etc. Resilient buildings are part of the overall package of development that cities need to consider in order to be prepared and be able to respond to particular events. The relationship of buildings to the infrastructure system and services as a whole and its ability to cope with particular events is often referred to as urban resilience. Individually and combined, the principal considerations relate to siting and potential exposure and risk. Green city development integrates these considerations into the overall planning process—strategic and detailed.

In Asian cities, the planning framework may not be sufficiently advanced, robust, or enforced to secure green and sustainable outcomes. Steps to improve such a situation will need to be taken through policy reform, technical support, and capacity building. However, at the same time, individual projects may provide an opportunity to act as demonstration project(s) to highlight good practice and principles of green and sustainable development, fulfilling two functions: improving green and promoting sustainable outcomes and capacity.

Green infrastructure is an integral element in the development of a sustainable built environment. While a relatively new concept for Asian cities, the opportunity for retrofitting and implementation of green infrastructure is great. In the context of Asian cities, green infrastructure provides a mechanism for improving resilience through measures such as improved drainage systems and open space networks. Similarly, green infrastructure considers energy use and the various ways by which efficiency can be improved, leading to reduced reliance on nonrenewable sources.

As a sector, and within the context of green cities, the built environment is significant. It highlights the interrelationships between sectors and how decisions taken at the site level have impacts at the city level and national level. It also highlights how integrated planning can act as the policy mechanism to manage that. In Asian cities, retrofitting may provide the first step toward implementing green infrastructure. The most common and obvious opportunity in Asian cities is around drainage systems and improving these through solid waste management, improved surface areas, and incorporation of natural filtration systems. In many circumstances, drains are covered over, clogged with refuse, and detention basins filled in. Incorporating SuDS and improving enforcement capacity can help remedy this situation but need to be in parallel with ongoing capacity building of municipal staff, and enforcement and operation and maintenance regimes.

Key Issues	Key Concepts
• Integrated land use planning • Urban resilience and adaptive capacity • Resilient buildings • Development control/compliance • Energy—renewable, low carbon • Land availability, access and orientation • Construction material, availability and sources • Thermal efficiency • Ecosystem services	• Risk-based planning • Green Infrastructure • Smart cities • Strategic planning • Retrofitting • SuDS • Compact city • Resilient buildings
Value-Added Options/Investment	
• Building code and rating system • Urban greening • Green, resilient infrastructure • Urban farming	• Alternative energy sources • Energy efficiency • Low-carbon transport • Smart cities
Available Resources	
• LEED • BREEAM • GREEN STAR • Tool for Rapid Assessment of City Energy	• UNEP: Liveable Cities • World Bank: Eco² Cities

Sector: Buildings and the Built Environment

Further Reading

- M. Lindfield and F. Steinberg, eds. 2012. *Green Cities*. Manila: Asian Development Bank. *A comprehensive and detailed publication on green cities.*
- S. Angel. 2012. *Planet of Cities*. Cambridge, MA.: Lincoln Institute of Land Policy.
- S. Reed, R. Friend, V. Toan, P. Thinphanga, R. Sutarto, and D. Singh. 2013. "Shared Learning" for Building Urban Climate Resilience—Experiences from Asian Cities.
- D. Dodman, D. Brown, K. Francis, J. Hardoy, C. Johson, and D. Satterwaite. 2013. Understanding the Nature and Scale of Urban Risk in Low-and Middle-Income Countries and its Implications for Humanitarian Preparedness, Planning and Response.
- Asian Development Bank. 2013. *Investing in Resilience: Ensuring a Disaster-Resistant Future*. Manila.
- A. K. Jha, T. W. Miner, and Z. Stanton-Geddes, eds. 2013. *Building Urban Resilience: Principles, Tools, and Practice. Directions in Development*. Washington, DC: World Bank.
- Natural England. 2013. Green Infrastructure—Valuation Tools Assessment.
- B. Madsen, N. Carroll, D. Kandy, and G. Bennett. 2011. *2011 Update: State of Biodiversity Markets*. Washington, DC: Forest Trends. Available at http://www. ecosystemmarketplace.com/reports/2011_update_sbdm
- B. Madsen, N. Carroll, and K. Moore Brands. 2010. *State of Biodiversity Markets Report: Offset and Compensation Programs Worldwide*. Washington, DC: Forest Trends. Available at http://www.ecosystemmarketplace.com/documents/acrobat/sbdmr.pdf

Crosscutting Themes and Considerations

- Energy
- Green infrastructure
- Climate change mitigation
- Climate change adaptation
- Sustainable land management
- Resilience

- Disaster risk
- Biodiversity
- Livelihoods
- Land use planning
- Low-carbon transport

2.10   Conceptualizing Integration

The key focus of this tool kit is to draw the sectors together to work out green city development interventions that support the attainment of green city principles. The key enabling factors for green city development include

- Policy and regulatory framework
- Strategic planning
- Links to finance

These elements are "enabling" because they provide an environment and development framework that supports green development. Once project and programs have been identified, the process of prioritization and investment planning commences. This process, along with respective enabling actions, supports a city to its transition and development as green and sustainable. This conceptual framework is set out in Figure 2.7.

Figure 2.7: Conceptual Framework Integrating Green City Development

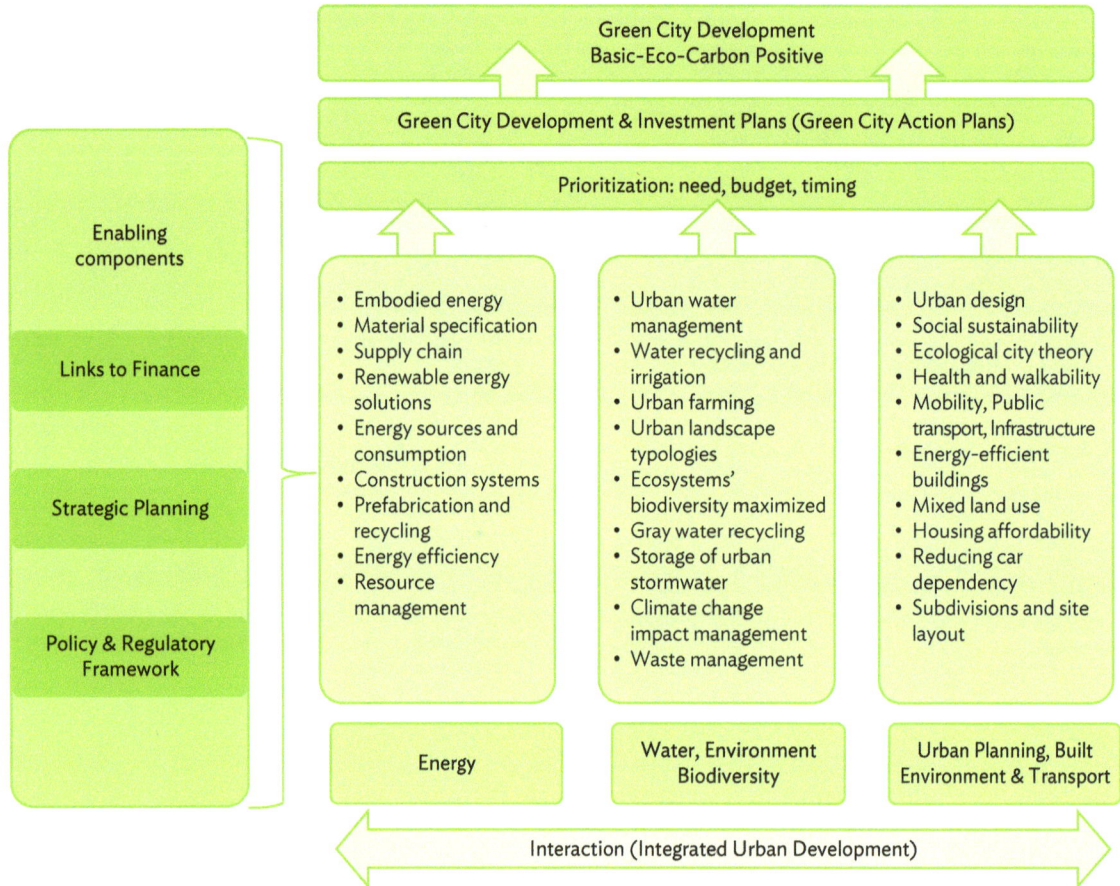

Green City Development Basic-Eco-Carbon Positive

Green City Development & Investment Plans (Green City Action Plans)

Prioritization: need, budget, timing

Enabling components

Links to Finance

Strategic Planning

Policy & Regulatory Framework

• Embodied energy • Material specification • Supply chain • Renewable energy solutions • Energy sources and consumption • Construction systems • Prefabrication and recycling • Energy efficiency • Resource management	• Urban water management • Water recycling and irrigation • Urban farming • Urban landscape typologies • Ecosystems' biodiversity maximized • Gray water recycling • Storage of urban stormwater • Climate change impact management • Waste management	• Urban design • Social sustainability • Ecological city theory • Health and walkability • Mobility, Public transport, Infrastructure • Energy-efficient buildings • Mixed land use • Housing affordability • Reducing car dependency • Subdivisions and site layout
Energy	**Water, Environment Biodiversity**	**Urban Planning, Built Environment & Transport**

Interaction (Integrated Urban Development)

Source: Emma Lewis adapted from Lehmann. 2010.

3. Green City Development: The Tool Kit

This tool kit is a reference guide for ADB staff and consultants, practitioners, and decision makers. It provides an accessible, practical, and comprehensive resource that signposts readers to available resources and introduces the fundamental building blocks and concepts for green city development. This document should not be viewed as static but as fluid and dynamic—in keeping with the transitional nature of cities and urban areas. Practice and experience will shape future approaches and reflect the iterative nature of urban development.

The preceding chapter introduced and explained green cities and their various components, highlighting key issues and concepts. This chapter explains the tool kit—a three-step framework for users to apply when considering green development in cities. The tool kit is not limited to studies of cities; the key concepts and approach can be applied at the national, regional, district, and neighborhood levels.

This tool kit functions across two levels: strategic and detailed. At the strategic level, it identifies key issues and development requirements to be addressed and situates a city within its current and desired green city status. It can, as explained in Figure 1.2, be used when formulating a country partnership, adopting the same approach but widening the geographical context. At a detailed level, it allows issues and city-specific interventions or actions to be identified and designed, which enables green and sustainable planning and investment to occur. Both levels enable objectives and targets to be set, which forms the basis for monitoring and evaluation frameworks enabling a feedback loop to be captured and the iterative nature of green urban development reflected.

The tool kit has been prepared in line with a standard program and project cycle that is consistent with the ADB project cycle. Figure 1.2 sets out this relationship. It supports ADB staff in their role in assisting DMCs in the preparation and implementation of green urban development plans.

The green city development tool kit (Figure 3.1) includes three steps that will guide users through a logical and analytical process to determine where a city currently is on the green development curve and what interventions could be made to improve green and sustainable outcomes in cities. The structure of the tool kit is such that the output of each step provides a technical input to the next step and, ultimately, assists in the design and selection of specific green city interventions. It also means that, in some instances, the outputs of a step will differ from those of specific assessments.

Expected Outcomes

The framework supports users to

- Undertake a situational analysis of a city to enable categorization within the green city framework (basic–eco–carbon positive);
- Identify and quantify system and sector-specific issues and improvement needs;
- Identify crosscutting themes and incorporate these issues across sectors and at the city level;
- Develop monitoring and evaluation frameworks to track progress;
- Prepare urban programs and projects that reflect green city objectives;

Figure 3.1: Green City Development Framework

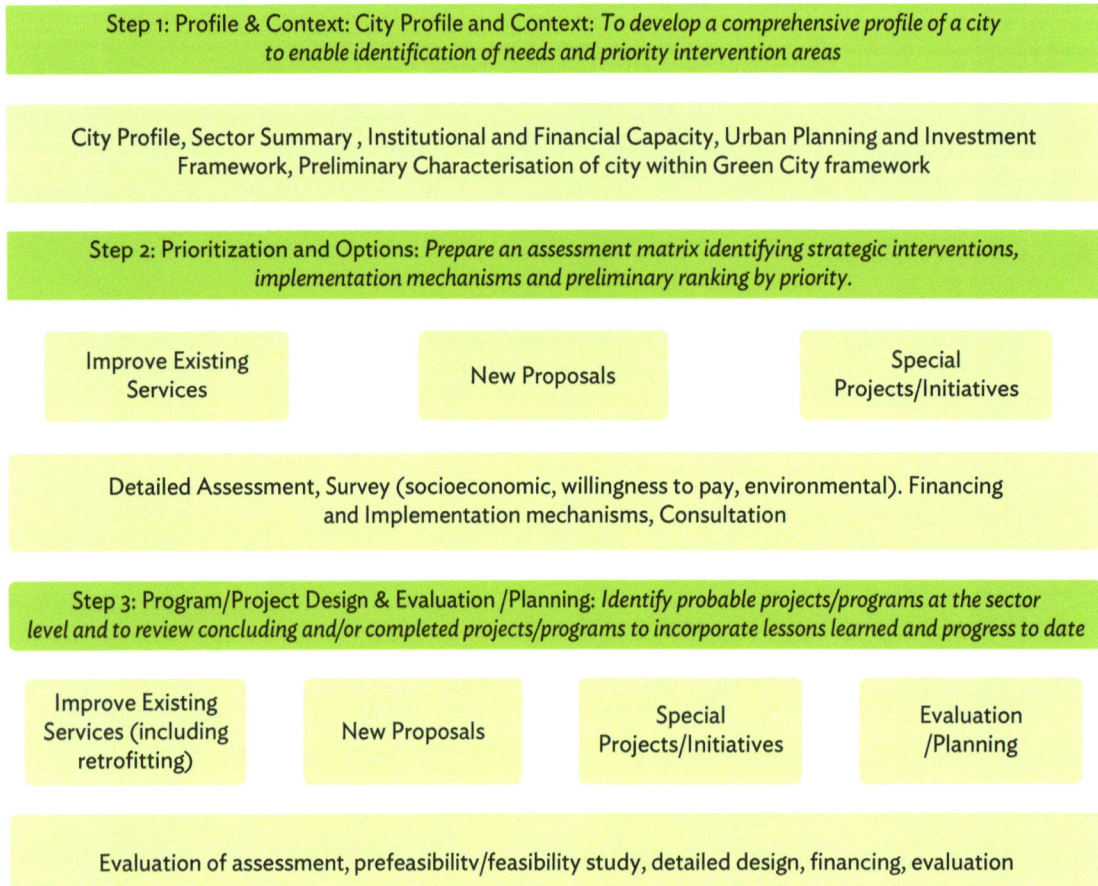

Step 1: Profile & Context: City Profile and Context: *To develop a comprehensive profile of a city to enable identification of needs and priority intervention areas*

City Profile, Sector Summary , Institutional and Financial Capacity, Urban Planning and Investment Framework, Preliminary Characterisation of city within Green City framework

Step 2: Prioritization and Options: *Prepare an assessment matrix identifying strategic interventions, implementation mechanisms and preliminary ranking by priority.*

Improve Existing Services	New Proposals	Special Projects/Initiatives

Detailed Assessment, Survey (socioeconomic, willingness to pay, environmental). Financing and Implementation mechanisms, Consultation

Step 3: Program/Project Design & Evaluation /Planning: *Identify probable projects/programs at the sector level and to review concluding and/or completed projects/programs to incorporate lessons learned and progress to date*

Improve Existing Services (including retrofitting)	New Proposals	Special Projects/Initiatives	Evaluation /Planning

Evaluation of assessment, prefeasibilitv/feasibility study, detailed design, financing, evaluation

Source: Emma Lewis.

- Identify institutional, fiscal, and regulatory support and reforms required to enable sectoral integration and facilitate green city objectives;
- Recognize capacity and current position on development and green city development curve considering issues such as data availability, governance, and decision-making frameworks, and develop responsive green city program and projects;
- Prioritize city-level and sector interventions underpinned by an understanding of sectoral linkages and opportunity for integrated green urban development;
- Prepare an outline or conceptual Green City Action Plan; and
- Improve terms of reference prepared for consultants engaged on green city projects through improved understanding of issues and requirements.

3.1   Step 1: City Profile and Context

Figure 3.2: Step 1 Summary

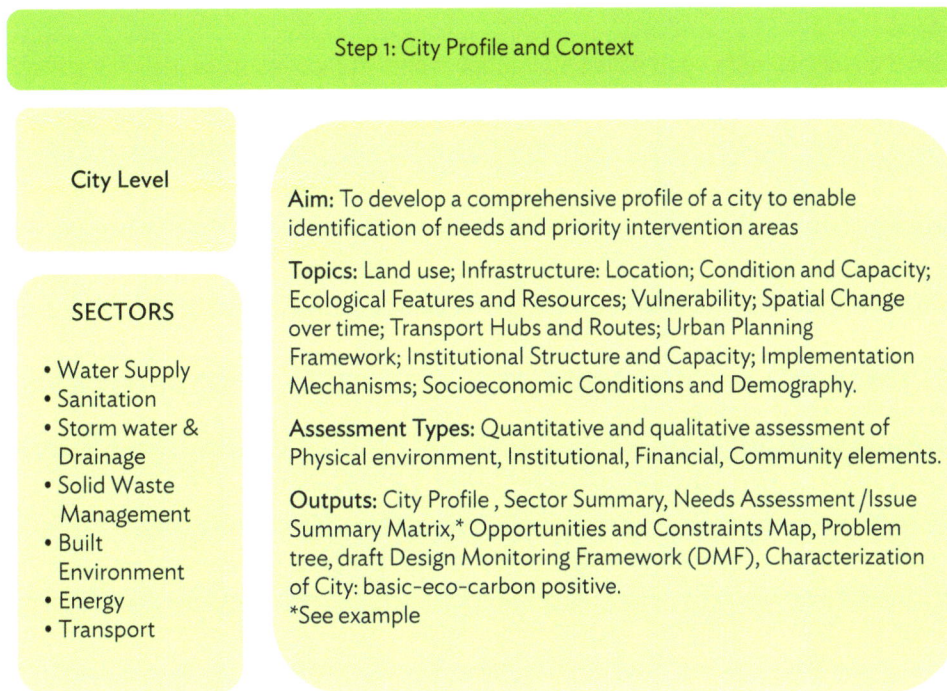

Step 1: City Profile and Context

City Level

SECTORS

- Water Supply
- Sanitation
- Storm water & Drainage
- Solid Waste Management
- Built Environment
- Energy
- Transport

Aim: To develop a comprehensive profile of a city to enable identification of needs and priority intervention areas

Topics: Land use; Infrastructure: Location; Condition and Capacity; Ecological Features and Resources; Vulnerability; Spatial Change over time; Transport Hubs and Routes; Urban Planning Framework; Institutional Structure and Capacity; Implementation Mechanisms; Socioeconomic Conditions and Demography.

Assessment Types: Quantitative and qualitative assessment of Physical environment, Institutional, Financial, Community elements.

Outputs: City Profile , Sector Summary, Needs Assessment /Issue Summary Matrix,* Opportunities and Constraints Map, Problem tree, draft Design Monitoring Framework (DMF), Characterization of City: basic-eco-carbon positive.
*See example

Source: Emma Lewis.

Step 1 provides the foundation for all subsequent steps to follow. It involves assessments at the city and sector levels. The primary output comprises a city profile and needs assessment matrix. A preliminary problem tree, and design and monitoring framework (DMF) are also prepared at this stage.

Tasks undertaken during Step 1 are significant and represent a large component of the work required within the three steps. This first step is crucial to developing an understanding of a city and identifying key issues.

Getting Started: Key Questions and Assessment Parameters

The first important question that needs to be considered when commencing is

- What are the basic elements that need to be in place to provide a platform for green cities to develop?

To answer this and adopting an integrated development approach, basic environmental infrastructure must be in place. This means that water supply and sanitation, in conjunction with basic solid waste management, must be considered together and in operation in some way.

Accordingly, all city assessments need to commence by establishing a base line (environmental and social). This process is reflected in Step 1, but it is important to stress here that establishing a baseline should not be a preoccupation when collating empirical data. In many Asian countries, data are scarce and unreliable. Thus, undertaking a green city assessment would require a pragmatic approach.

A starting point to begin building a profile and understanding of a city is to ask several basic questions:

- What is the spatial extent of the area being assessed? How does this relate to other or nearby centers?
- What are the predominant land use(s), and where are they located?
- What are its natural features?
- What are the available urban services?
- What are the major environmental challenges (air pollution, water pollution, sea-level rise, etc.)?
- Why is green development relevant to the city?

These initial questions are then supplemented by more detailed questions that will include

- What are the relevant legislative and policy frameworks? Are there any changes proposed, and when were the last changes made? Who is responsible for administering respective frameworks?
- What is the nature of the planning system(s)?
- Who are the service providers, and what are their size and capacity?
- Who are the key stakeholders?
- What are the needs of the community?
- What are the existing plans?
- What are the available data and who is responsible for maintaining such data?
- What are the thrust areas or core sectors that will catalyze green city development?
- What is the relationship and extent to which (a city's) respective management policies, plans, programs, and projects influence priorities and pathways of growth, including livelihoods and their direct impact on the quality of life?
- What are the tools predominantly used to assess the qualitative and quantitative profiles of these sectors and, in turn, their impacts across and within sectors?
- What is the architecture of regulations and fiscal, nonfiscal, and market-based instruments that will enable stakeholders to comply with benchmarks of environmental and resource efficiency?

The preparation of the tool kit is founded on the importance of developing interventions that are locally relevant and adapted to the specific nature of a city. Step 1 of the tool kit supports this position by recommending the preparation of a detailed city profile that explores the physical elements of a city as well as the institutional and community elements along with the availability and access to empirical data.

This first step is an assessment or "scan" of available resources and conditions, and is undertaken to provide context and summary of issues.

**Box 1: Viet Nam Secondary Cities Development Program (Green Cities) –
Green City Development in Action**

Approved in June 2014, the Concept Paper[11] for this assignment sets out how the concept of green city development will be implemented in Viet Nam. An innovative program, the Secondary Cities Development Program proposes a results-based loan and administration of grant funding. In its preparatory phase, the program will enable the development of sustainable and resource-efficient urban growth models for secondary cities in Viet Nam. With a focus on integrating sectors and preparation of green city action plans to support Viet Nam's green growth strategy, the program will see a strong collaboration between experts from the government, the Asian Development Bank, and the prospective team of consultants.

---

[11]   ADB. 2014. Proposed Results-Based Loan and Administration of Grant Socialist Republic of Viet Nam: Secondary Cities Development Program (Green Cities) Concept Paper.

Source: Concept Paper.

City Profile

A city profile provides a summary of existing conditions and features of a city. It includes institutional arrangements, development plans, availability and extent of urban infrastructure and services, and a summary of environmental conditions. Figure 3.3 shows an example of a template that can be used and adapted when preparing a city profile. It is complemented with a social profile that provides greater detail about the characteristics of a city's population (see section 3.2.4 Social Profile).

Figure 3.3: Example of City Profile Template

General Information			
Name of City			
Type of Municipality			
Year Established			
District			
State			
Country			
Location and Climate			
Geographical Position of the City			
Type of Climate			
Temperature– Average			
Average Rainfall/Precipitation (millimeter)			
Number of Rainy Days			
Average Humidity			
Average Wind speed			
Area and Population (Note: A separate social profile should be prepared to complement this section.)			
Area (square kilometer)			
Population			
Decadal Population Growth Rate (%)			
Population Density			
Land Use Composition (%)			
	Current (%)		Proposed (%)
	YEAR		YEAR
Residential			
Commercial			
Industrial			
Education and Public Purpose			
Open and Recreation			
Roads and Railway			

Vacant Land		
Agriculture		
Water Bodies		

Ecological/Natural Features			
	Location	Area/Extent	Condition
		Identify also if cross-boundary	*Information needed/obtained to make assessment*

Financial Profile		
Currency	YEAR	YEAR
Local/Own Source Income	*Records received should cover 5-year period.*	
Central Transfers		
Capital Receipts		
Borrowing		
Total Income		
Operating Expenditure		
Repairs and Maintenance Expenditure		
Capital Expenditure		
Debt Servicing		
Total Expenditure		
Outstanding Debts		
Debt Service Ratio		

City (Infrastructure Services)	
Water Availability	
Installed Capacity (million gallons per day)	
Released/daily (million gallons per day)	
Source of Water Supply	
Within City Limits	
10–50 square kilometers	
50–100 square kilometers	
Water Coverage	
Population covered by water supply (%)	
Per capita supply (liters per capita per day)	
Supply duration (liters per capita per day)	
Wastewater Coverage	
Wastewater generated daily (million gallons per day)	
Disposal capacity (million gallons per day)	
Present operating capacity (million gallons per day)	

Households connected to underground sewerage collection (%)	
Solid Waste	
Waste generation daily (tons per day)	
Collection daily (tons per day)	
Stormwater Drainage	
Annual rainfall	
Length of stormwater drains (kilometer)	
Road and Transport	
Municipal roads (kilometer)	
State-level roads (kilometer)	
Public Transport	
Buses/Train/Others Number	
Capacity/Passengers	
Private Registered Vehicles	
Housing[12]	
Number of households	
Number of housing units	
Number or households in slums/informal settlements	
Housing backlog	
Green Initiatives	
Project/Programs/Policies	*(List and highlight key features.)*
Land Use Planning and Urban Management System	
Identify existing and proposed plans	Year, status
Disaster Management and Mitigation	
Identify existing and proposed plans and development initiatives	Year, status, allocated budget (implementation)

The example can be adjusted and tailored to each area and expanded to capture more detailed information about a specific section, as required. A city profile may be kept in tabular form as a means of presenting information in a simple and clear manner. This profile will form the basis for more detailed assessments to be undertaken (Step 2).

Social Profile

A city profile also needs to include information about the community and resident population. This will take the form of a social profile. An initial social profile should be prepared based on the available information. More detailed information will be gathered and assessed under Step 2.

---

[12]   For more detailed guidance on preparing a housing profile, see UN-Habitat. 2010. A Practical Guide for Conducting: Housing Profiles. http://www.unhabitat.org/pmss/listItemDetails.aspx?publicationID=3158

A social profile provides a summary of a city's demographics, i.e., the characteristics of a population. Data may include

- Gender
- Age
- Education level
- Ethnicity
- Employment status
- Income

Often, such data are collected by a census, which is a systematic survey designed to find out about the whole population of a given country. The data provide the basis for preparing a socioeconomic profile of the different areas of the city and to identify at-risk and vulnerable communities. The social profile prepared under Step 1 provides the basis for more detailed survey(s) and is undertaken under Step 2.

The social profile is an important component within the ADB project cycle particularly in the conduct of a poverty and social analysis. An initial poverty and social analysis is undertaken during the early stages of a project preparatory technical assistance to enable early identification of persons who may be beneficially or adversely affected by the project.

For further guidance on poverty and social analysis, and in relation to the ADB project cycle, refer to Asian Development Bank. 2012. *Handbook on Poverty and Social Analysis: A Working Document.*

Building the City Profile

In this tool kit, four thematic areas form the basis for identifying programs and projects. These are:

- Environment/Resource Management
- Policy and governance
- Financial framework
- Project implementation mechanism

The information obtained while preparing the city profile can be structured within these four themes and used as a basis for identifying gaps in information, service delivery, and overall performance and will be presented in a needs assessment (see next section).

• Environment/Resource Management

Prepare a summary and assessment of all ecological features that are present within the city, what condition they are in, and what uses they fulfill. This assessment can be in the form of an inventory and presented spatially via a natural features (and hazards) map. The aim is to establish the baseline conditions of a city and, through review of available data, ascertain what change has occurred over time, and what (if any) negative and positive effects have been experienced or observed.

An opportunities and constraints map can also be prepared at this stage. This presents information spatially and identifies features and areas that require specific consideration. It includes land suitability for development, cross-boundary or administrative issues and connectivity, future development areas or plans, and flood-prone and/or hazardous areas.

An opportunities and constraints map is a practical output that can be the basis for community engagement. It is a simplified way to present multiple data and obtain feedback (particularly in hazardous areas) on the extent of impact of particular events within communities. An opportunities and constraints map will be updated under Step 2.

• Policy and governance

Prepare a summary of relevant institutional stakeholders and present this graphically. A mapping exercise can also be undertaken to highlight relationships and decision-making processes. This step should identify key stakeholders in the urban sector and establish the decision-making framework(s). It also includes identifying all relevant legislation and policy.

• Financial framework

As with policy and governance, a similar assessment is required to map out the city's financial framework and how this is linked to decision making. A preliminary assessment of the city's statements of income and expenditure (over the last 10 years) and previous and current 5-year investment plans (if available) will help ascertain toward what areas investment is directed, and help identify gaps and areas for improvement.

Based on city financial statements and the emerging issues from preparing the city profile, the assessment should begin to consider what alternative sources of finance may be available for the city.

• Project implementation mechanism

This parameter assesses what implementation mechanisms are currently employed by the city and at what stage (preparation, implementation, completion). This assessment should complement and support those assessments in policy, governance, and financial areas. The purpose of this assessment is to begin identifying implementation deficiencies and opportunities for improvement.

The city profile and combined summaries of each theme are not dissimilar to a *scoping report*, which sets out the broad parameters and interactions, preliminary findings, and, most importantly, identifies information gaps to be addressed in Steps 2 and 3. This assessment forms the foundation for Steps 2 and 3.

It should be noted that the city profile, and the subsequent needs assessment, identifies existing plans and policies, and where there are gaps or disconnects. The overarching objective of green city development is to harmonize these plans and planning processes to support an integrated approach.

Needs Assessment Matrix

Upon completion of the city profile, a needs assessment is undertaken to identify gaps in current conditions against a future desired condition. Figure 3.4 provides an example of needs assessment matrix that has been structured by sector and theme.

Figure 3.4: Needs Assessment Matrix

	Environment/ Resource Management	Policy and Governance	Financial Management	Implementation
Water Supply				
Sanitation				
Stormwater & Drainage				
Transport				
Solid Waste Management				
Built Environment				
Energy				
City Level				

Source: Emma Lewis.

The needs assessment is completed using the information contained in the city profile and thematic summaries. It is, in essence, a synthesis of all work undertaken under Step 1. The matrix is completed by filling in identified issues and requirements under each heading. This matrix will be further developed under Steps 2 and 3 based on additional information. This initial assessment forms the basis for the problem tree, and design and monitoring framework to be completed (see next section).

Problem Tree

Following the preparation of the city profile and needs analysis, it is possible to synthesize this information into a problem tree. A problem tree is a form of situational analysis that is useful for highlighting the relationships and linkages between complex issues. Such an analysis is particularly useful for urban development projects as it enables issues to be placed in a hierarchy of related factors, that is, it can be used to link together various issues that may contribute to a problem. Figure 3.5 below provides a problem tree outline. A problem tree forms the basis of a logical framework (log frame)/ design and monitoring framework that is explained in the following section.

Figure 3.5: Problem Tree

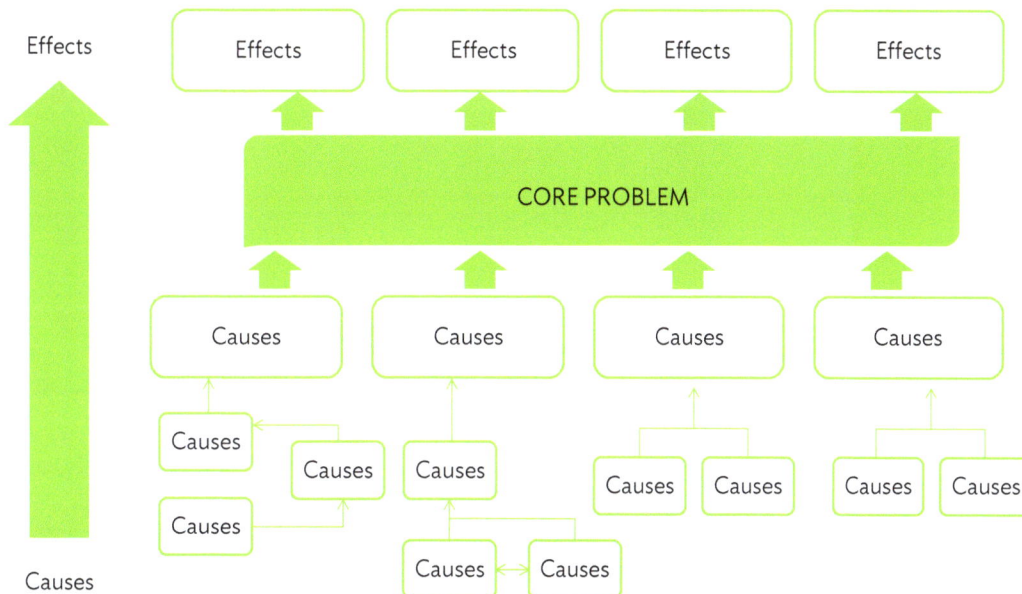

Effects

| Effects | Effects | Effects | Effects |

CORE PROBLEM

| Causes | Causes | Causes | Causes |

Causes, Causes, Causes, Causes, Causes, Causes, Causes, Causes, Causes, Causes

Causes

Source: Adapted from ADB Guidelines for preparing a design and monitoring framework, July 2007 second edition.

Design and Monitoring Framework (Logical Framework)

A logical framework (log frame) is, in ADB parlance, a design and monitoring framework (DMF). A key component of any program or project, a log frame is results oriented and provides an analytical framework that helps users to conceptualize, design, implement, monitor, and evaluate projects.

A log frame uses a matrix to clearly explain the impact, outcome, and outputs of a program/project. The project *impact* captures the broader "why" and the *outcome* sets out the desired change. It is followed by a series of outputs or deliverables that are supported by a description of process (i.e., the activities that turn inputs into outputs) and inputs (total resource financial and time) in order to achieve the impact. A log frame is an expression of a "Results Chain" (Figure 3.6), which is the framework setting out what the program or project is expected to achieve.

Figure 3.6: Results Chain

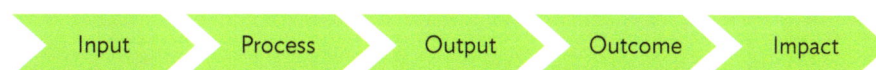

Input > Process > Output > Outcome > Impact

Source: DFID Practice Paper. 2011.

Figure 3.7: Example of Design and Monitoring Framework Matrix

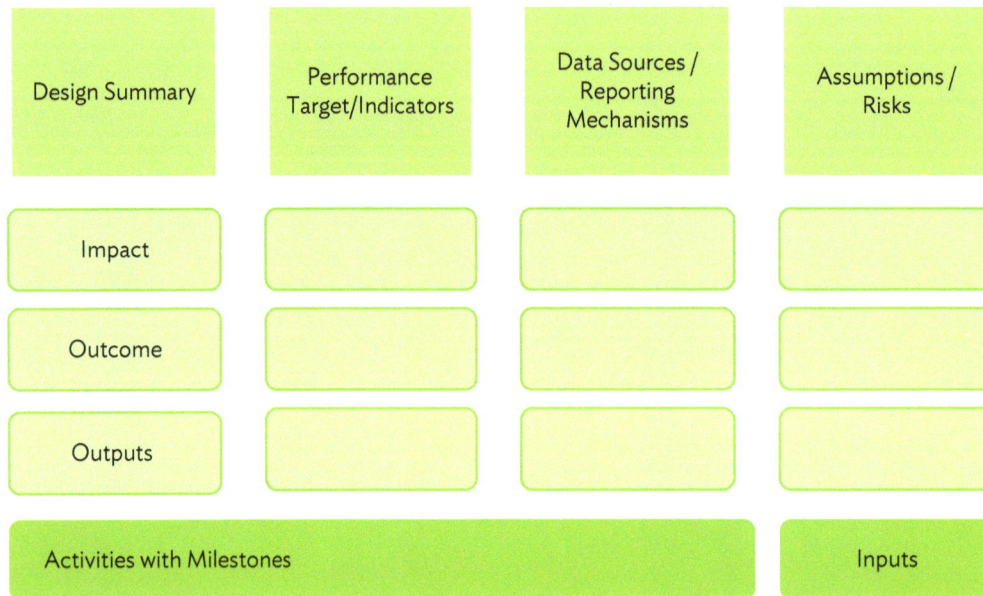

Design Summary	Performance Target/Indicators	Data Sources / Reporting Mechanisms	Assumptions / Risks
Impact			
Outcome			
Outputs			
Activities with Milestones			Inputs

Source: Adapted from ADB Guidelines for preparing a design and monitoring framework, July 2007 second edition.

The multisector nature of "urban" projects means that developing a log frame can be challenging. Despite its challenges, developing a log frame early in the process is a good way of working through what the key issues are in developing a preliminary project outline.

Following the problem tree analysis, it is possible to begin completing the DMF matrix. The matrix, as set out in Figure 3.7, is the principal means of articulating what a project sets out to achieve, and what is required to enable that.

Completing the log frame is iterative and develops further as a project or program's design develops or as a result of an evaluation at review points during the lifetime of a project. A log frame is based on a cause-and-effect relationship, and a good way to ascertain if a project is *logical* is to consider the following:

> IF we undertake the activities AND the assumptions hold true,
>
> THEN we will create the outputs.
>
> IF we deliver the outputs AND the assumptions hold true,
>
> THEN we will achieve the outcome.
>
> IF we achieve the outcome AND the assumptions hold true,
>
> THEN we will contribute to the impact.

Source: DFID Practice Paper. 2011.

Within the context of Green Cities, this logic does not change. It is necessary to consider how any proposed intervention will achieve the desired impact, what support and resources are needed, and what assumptions have been made.

For multisector projects as Green City development will predominantly be, the focus will invariably center on *outcomes*. The impact may be easier to articulate, but it is the outcomes that will begin to frame the interplay between sectors. For example, the outcomes will separate the needs in, say, provision of basic infrastructure and the need to improve land use planning capacity. As such, there will need to be outcome themes identifying the anticipated outputs and inputs required. These two elements form subprojects or components within the main project, but *together* will enable the impact to be realized.

Another useful tool for use in log frames is SMART objectives. This stands for specific, measurable, achievable, results-oriented, and time-bound and is a way of developing project objectives to facilitate maximum impact.

Log Frames and Indicators

Identifying and preparing indicators is a key element of a monitoring and evaluation framework; it allows targets to be set and progress to be tracked. It is important to note the various tiers of evaluation.

The key element differentiating indicators with other types of data is the connectivity with policy: indicators and policy are linked, or should be linked, in a very explicit manner. This implies that during the creation of an indicator, as compared to purely statistical exercises, a considerable amount of time and effort is put into establishing what type of data collection is needed. However, it is important to highlight that indicators are not data; rather, they are models that allow the simplification of a complex issue to a few numbers that can be easily comprehended by policymakers and the wider public.

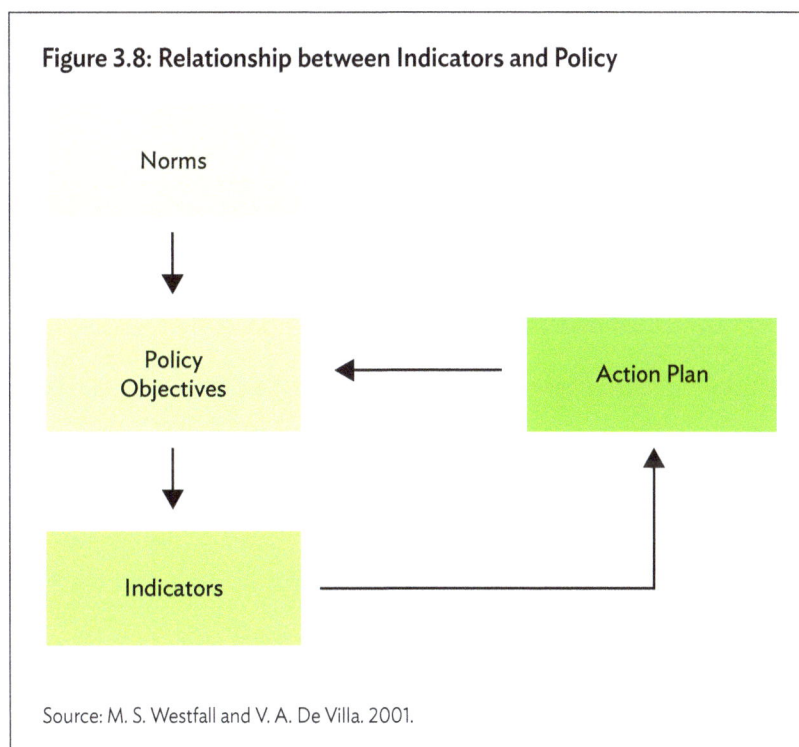

Figure 3.8: Relationship between Indicators and Policy

Norms

Policy Objectives

Action Plan

Indicators

Source: M. S. Westfall and V. A. De Villa. 2001.

Indicators and policy are thus closely intertwined: a core objective is to attain the seamless incorporation of indicators with policy; policy is supported by indicators, and indicators would not come to be without policy. Indicators and strategic planning thus have a symbiotic relationship: once policy is designed and priorities are set, indicators can be established to serve as a benchmark; they allow assessing progress toward the objectives. Figure 3.8 illustrates the relationship between indicators and policy.

In this context, indicators of green city investment would allow tracking the various efforts that Asian cities undertake in their quest toward sustainability. Establishing indicators of green city investment would thus mean measuring the success of policy efforts and interventions aiming at promoting sustainability. Green city indicators allow feeding the policy process by evaluating what actions are successful in the improvement of livability and minimization of environmental impacts. Green city indicators therefore have the potential to provide invaluable insight(s) into whether strategic planning or city action plan designed to attain or ensure sustainability is actually working, and whether the actions are based on sound premises.

Methodological guidelines

The methodology designed and followed to establish indicators is a major emerging issue. The idea of a "green" city is not necessarily directly observable; it is a broad theme characterized by its **multidimensional** nature. The difficulty lies in establishing a methodology that gives a true account of the multidimensional aspect, and allows incorporating into a single indicator—referred to as index—all the different elements (and their attached indicators) comprising the broad theme. The data triangle (Figure 3.9) illustrates the various existing types of data.

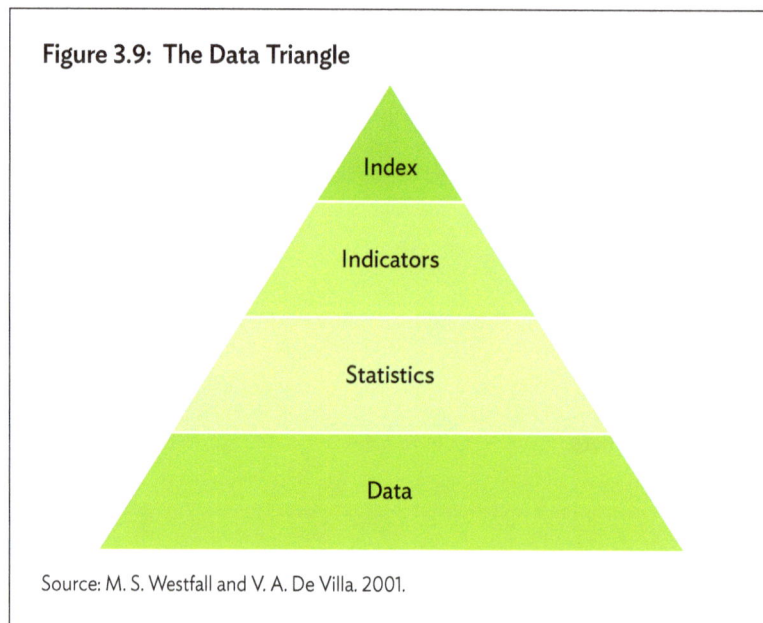

Figure 3.9: The Data Triangle

Index

Indicators

Statistics

Data

Source: M. S. Westfall and V. A. De Villa. 2001.

Ultimately, a goal for city governments may be to construct a green city index to enable progress and comparison across multiple urban areas to occur. An existing example of an index is the Asian Green City Index.[13] This index proposes eight categories (for evaluation): energy and carbon dioxide, land use and buildings, transport, waste, water, sanitation, air quality, and environmental governance. Within these categories, 29 indicators are identified. Indicators can be either quantitative (assessing how a city actually performs) or qualitative (evaluating policies and plans).

This index provides a well-documented and well-considered methodology for preparing an index. However, as noted, the availability of data is a major challenge particularly in many Asian cities where data are not yet captured, stored, processed, or available. Thus, in selecting indicators and determining categories for evaluation, it is important to consider the transitional nature of cities and development trajectory.[14] Technical and financial capacity to gather, process, share, and maintain data across cities will differ. Accordingly, while evaluation categories may be determined upfront and retained across multiple periods, selected indicators may change or, put differently, the data gaps are known and overtime actions undertaken to remedy this and thus collect relevant data to enable a specific indicator to be used.

The construction of an index with various categories and their attached indicators is thus the effect of a sound process of progression: as a city moves forward in terms of economic and social development, this can be accompanied by an enhancement in its capabilities for measuring the achievement of sustainability objectives. Simultaneously, with an improvement of overall living conditions, higher sustainability targets can be set and, if data availability and processing advances as well, these targets can be better tracked and accounted for.

The initial DMF prepared during Step 1 will frame the type of indicators to be used and will enable evaluation elements to be "built in" to the project design. Both Steps 2 and 3 will update and refer to the DMF; the problem tree analysis and completion of the DMF are very important aspects to support green city development.

Crosscutting Themes

The problem tree and the DMF prepared during Step 1 help structure problems, causes, and objectives, and consider interventions through a multisector prism. Understanding and identifying crosscutting issues is central to green city development. At this stage, issues arising from Step 1 can be considered in two broad categories—environmental and operational.

At the operational level, several elements apply across city or sector level. These include

- Forward planning
  - Access to land and land availability– how does this impact the proposed intervention?
  - Capacity planning – what are the future requirements? Is there scope for expansion (e.g., water treatment and supply facilities, transport)?

---

[13] The Asian Green City Index, developed by the Economist Intelligence Unit in partnership with Siemens, provides a good account of the emerging issues and challenges to construct a methodology for evaluating the achievements of Asian cities in the attainment or promotion of sustainability. In order to construct the index, data were gathered from April to June 2010; across all major Asian countries, 22 cities were selected based on their size and importance, and the selection sought to incorporate capital cities or cities of major commercial and business significance.

[14] See also S. Joss, ed. 2012. *Tomorrow's City Today: Eco-City Indicators, Standards & Frameworks. Bellagio Conference Report.* London: University of Westminster.

- Operation and Maintenance
    - Appropriate use of technology – cost, capacity, upkeep
    - Technical capacity – what exists and what is needed?

- Implementation models
    - Leveraging the private sector: public–private partnership, build–operate–transfer, build–own–operate–transfer, and design–build–operate–maintain.

At the environmental level, the following parameters provide a summary of some considerations and interrelationships:

- Energy usage and carbon dioxide emissions can be calculated per capita and energy consumption per unit of GDP; these indicators influence clean energy policy and preparation of local action plans to tackle impacts due to climate change.
- Population density, specifically floor area ratios as reflected in land use and building policy, is related also to determining green space per capita and green corridor networks.
- Public transport network(s), congestion reduction policies (and potential levies), and viable mass transit systems that consider alternative fuels and technology as mechanisms to improve efficiency are important parameters in the transport sector.
- Waste: volume collected and disposal requirement, use of technology and alternative energy and revenue streams via waste-to-energy, methane capture considered within the context of recycling and composting options per capita and use policy, the quantum collected and method and technology used for disposal and its relationship to recycling capacity and per capita waste generation.
- Water-related parameters include water consumption per capita, system leakages, quality and sustainability aspects including extraction and the influence of mitigation policies.
- Sanitation parameters include the proportion of population that has access to such services, the location and condition of pipe network and system leakages, location of treatment facility, access to the facility, geography (such as watercourses), and climate.
- Air pollution and air quality within cities are the parameters linked to land use (including energy required for operation), transport planning, and consideration to these interconnections will influence mitigation and adaptation responses.
- Environmental governance includes management, monitoring, public participation, reporting, and performance of technologies for abatement.
- Aspects of green economy include job creation, attractiveness of business, retention incentives, renewable energy portfolio standards, retrofit incentives, recycling regulation, venture capital fund, cluster initiatives, brownfield remediation, and high-density development, in addition to capacity building for the future.
- Influence and enforcement of compliance regulations including market mechanisms to provide incentives to promote compliance and the need to consider unintended consequences or potential negative impacts as a result of any financial incentives offered.

3.2   Step 2: Prioritization and Options

Figure 3.10: Step 2 Summary

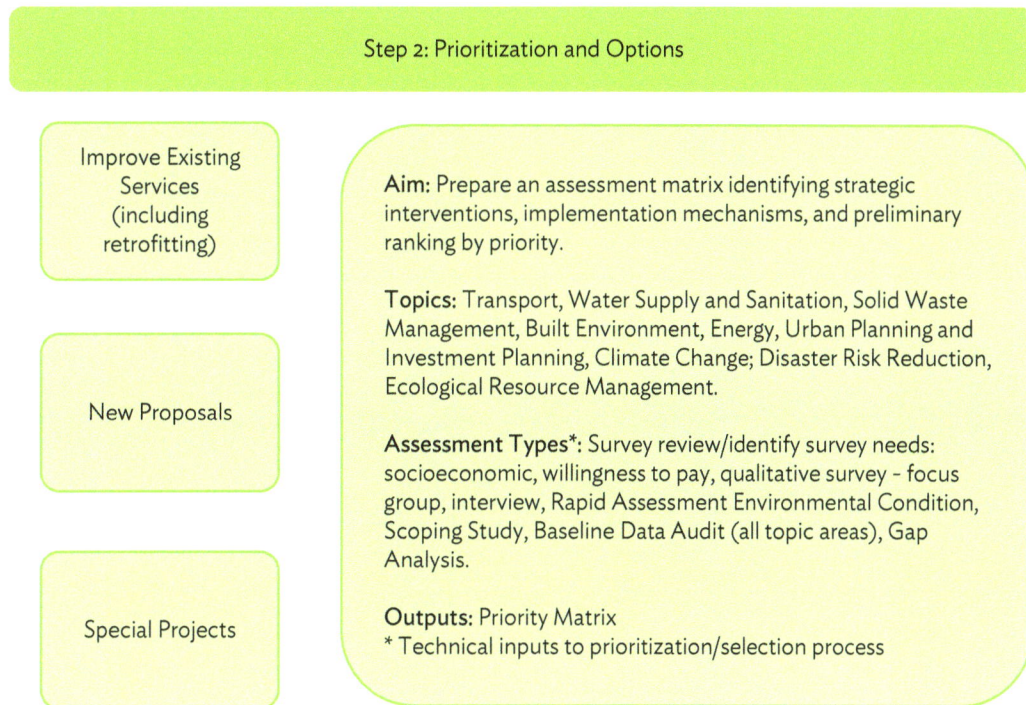

Step 2: Prioritization and Options

Improve Existing Services (including retrofitting)

New Proposals

Special Projects

Aim: Prepare an assessment matrix identifying strategic interventions, implementation mechanisms, and preliminary ranking by priority.

Topics: Transport, Water Supply and Sanitation, Solid Waste Management, Built Environment, Energy, Urban Planning and Investment Planning, Climate Change; Disaster Risk Reduction, Ecological Resource Management.

Assessment Types*: Survey review/identify survey needs: socioeconomic, willingness to pay, qualitative survey - focus group, interview, Rapid Assessment Environmental Condition, Scoping Study, Baseline Data Audit (all topic areas), Gap Analysis.

Outputs: Priority Matrix
* Technical inputs to prioritization/selection process

Source: Emma Lewis.

Step 2 of the tool kit identifies priority investments areas and options for a city to become, improve, and adapt to green and sustainable city principles.

Step 2 builds on the information and initial assessments undertaken during Step 1 and, in particular, the identified information gaps. Step 2 takes this work forward by conducting a more detailed gap analysis (reference to the problem tree will assist this process). The output of the gap analysis is twofold. First, it highlights current deficiencies in green city investment (infrastructure, service delivery, resources, etc.); and second, it highlights where information or data is absent and what additional work is required to enable robust decision making and investment programming. It also works across two levels: strategic and detailed or sector specific. This is important as the tool kit is applied and is relevant to both—it is the relationship between each that enables the realization of green city development.

Within the ADB project cycle, Step 2 is undertaken during the "preparation" phase (see Figure 1.2). The identified projects should be consistent with the focus areas of the respective country's partnership strategy. Thus, under Step 2, key areas have already been identified from the country partnership strategy; a profile and contextualization completed under Step 1; and now, Step 2 requires information gaps to be filled, feasibility study to be undertaken, and prioritization of projects completed. This process (applied at the project level) will be the most common application of the tool kit. However, the tool kit is also applicable at the strategic level. In relation to the ADB project cycle, Step 1 can be applied for county-level assessment to inform the preparation of the country partnership strategy. Step 2 will then prioritize across sector and geography to highlight focal points.

Under Step 2, a range of additional investigations may be undertaken. Figure 3.10 highlights the assessments that may be undertaken, and this includes survey work. As highlighted, Step 2 is undertaken during the "preparation" phase of the ADB project cycle. The most common survey required is a socioeconomic survey, which enables a more detailed picture of a community to be obtained. Often, this will also include a willingness-to-pay survey. This survey helps identify and define affordability issues and willingness to pay for particular services. In the context of green city development and its multisector nature, this can help develop interventions that respond to a community's need for basic services; enable a solid platform for development on a green and sustainable trajectory; and situate this within considerations of affordability, revenue generation, and future investment areas.

Priority Matrix

The objective of Step 2 is to prepare a priority list of projects. To assist with this process, a priority matrix can be prepared. A priority matrix is a summary of possible projects across sector and theme, and is based on Step 1 and additional assessments completed under Step 2. It is a tool that is used for project and investment planning.

The priority matrix outlined in Figure 3.11 includes three thematic areas for investment:

- **Improvement of existing services**
  Identification of how existing urban service(s) can be improved or upgraded in line with green city principles—including retrofitting.

- **New proposals**
  Focuses on sector-specific new project proposals or programs that can help the city become more "green."

- **Special projects (investments and reforms)**
  Identification of special interventions—may include strategic infrastructure, legislative, financial, and policy reforms.

Prioritization

Two principal factors determine priorities: need and financial capacity. Steps 1 and 2 have determined the needs of a city. Information on the financial capacity of the city will have been obtained during this phase (but may require more detailed assessments to be undertaken). The process of prioritizing now draws these two elements together. The Cities Development Initiative for Asia (CDIA) publication, *City Infrastructure Investment Programming and Prioritisation Toolkit,*[15] is an accessible and practical guide that explains the prioritization process in detail (the summary of the approach is provided in Box 2).

---

[15]   Cities Development Initiative for Asia website. http://www.cdia.asia/knowledge-materials/ciipp-toolkit/

Box 2: Cities Development Initiative for Asia: Three Steps for Prioritization

Step 1 – Analysis of the city/local government's financial condition and capacity to finance future capital projects

It comprises a (quantitative) assessment of the municipality's fiscal data as well as a (qualitative) assessment of the financial management capacity. The data are used to make a projection of the local budget available for investment.

Step 2 – Assessment of the quality of proposed projects

Uses both qualitative and quantitative data. It requires input from a variety of people and agencies within the city administration. The prioritization exercise results in a shortlist of projects.

Step 3 – Investment packages

Based on the outcomes of Steps 1 and 2, develop investment packages with a 5-year horizon.

Source: Cities Development Initiative for Asia. 2014.

Figure 3.11: Priority Matrix

Sector	Improve Existing Services				New Projects				Special Interventions			
	Environment	Policy and Governance	Financial	Implementation	Environment	Policy and Governance	Financial	Implementation	Environment	Policy and Governance	Financial	Implementation
Water Supply												
Sanitation												
Stormwater & Drainage												
Transport												
Solid Waste management												
Built Environment												
Energy												
City Level												

Source: Emma Lewis.

Figure 3.12: Traffic Light Rating System

🔴	Inadequate/poor, high risk, behind schedule
🟡	Reasonable, moderate risk, partially behind schedule
🟢	Good, low risk, on schedule

This matrix can be simplified to provide a concise visual prompt of a city profile (focus areas) and adapted to form the basis of a scorecard to track progress. "Traffic light," a common and useful rating system that can be applied to any scorecard or reporting framework, uses red, amber, and green to highlight performance, progress, and risk (Figure 3.12).

3.3   Step 3: Design and Evaluation/Planning

Figure 3.13: Step 3 Summary

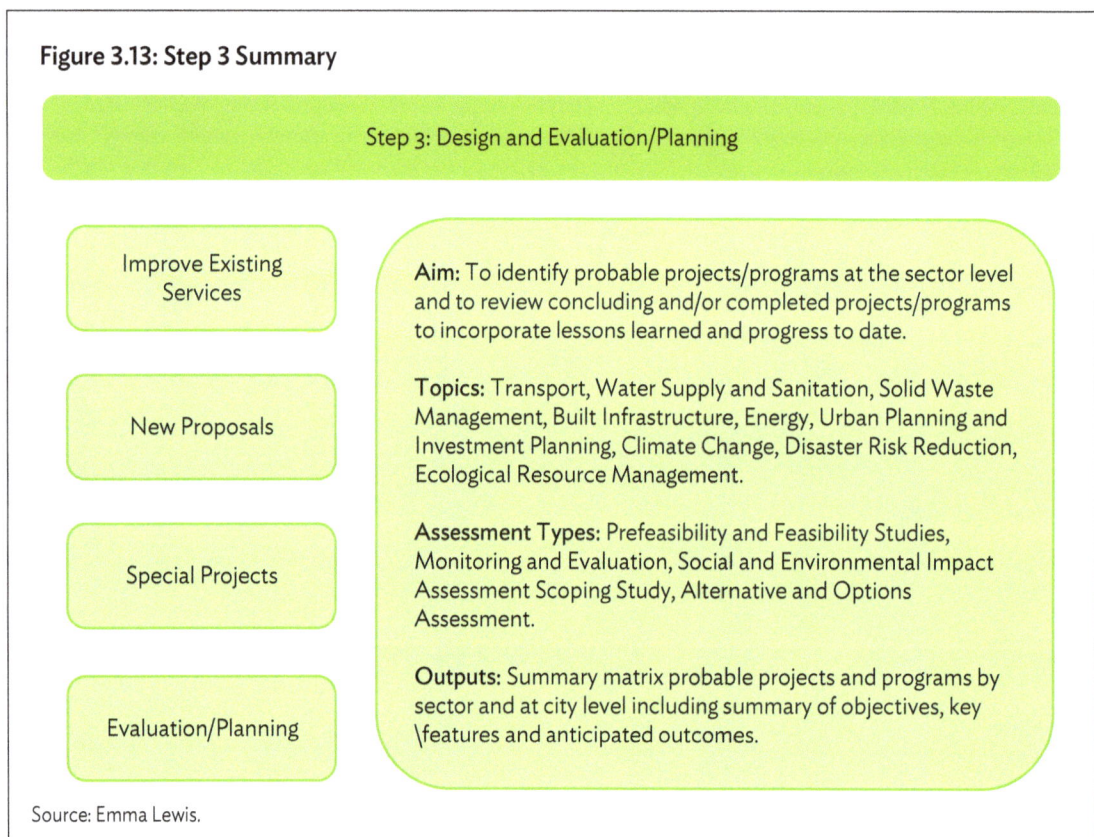

Step 3: Design and Evaluation/Planning

Improve Existing Services

New Proposals

Special Projects

Evaluation/Planning

Aim: To identify probable projects/programs at the sector level and to review concluding and/or completed projects/programs to incorporate lessons learned and progress to date.

Topics: Transport, Water Supply and Sanitation, Solid Waste Management, Built Infrastructure, Energy, Urban Planning and Investment Planning, Climate Change, Disaster Risk Reduction, Ecological Resource Management.

Assessment Types: Prefeasibility and Feasibility Studies, Monitoring and Evaluation, Social and Environmental Impact Assessment Scoping Study, Alternative and Options Assessment.

Outputs: Summary matrix probable projects and programs by sector and at city level including summary of objectives, key \features and anticipated outcomes.

Source: Emma Lewis.

Step 3 is the final step and begins to take identified priorities and issues and considers how to integrate development interventions to enable outcomes that support advancement of a green city. In practical terms, this means that, by Step 3 of the process, the preliminary investigations will have determined:

• the stage of "green city" development at the city and sector levels,
• as certained the status of basic environmental infrastructure (urban services), and
• identified the priority areas for intervention.

Step 3 is applied at several points during the ADB project cycle: during preparation, implementation, and evaluation stages.

Preparation

At preparation stage, Step 3 takes the work undertaken during the previous steps and considers how it can be progressed. It forms the final stage of the feasibility study that was commenced under Step 2, identifying and developing priority projects and subprojects. The preliminary problem tree and DMF are updated to reflect the studies and analyses undertaken during Steps 1 and 2. During this stage, project outlines and consultant terms of reference may be prepared. The terms of reference will

* provide a concise summary of the city profile, identifying key issues and rationale for green city development;
* identify the scope of works required in line with the preparatory work undertaken during previous steps;
* set out the requirements of the consultant team, identifying necessary skill sets and expected deliverables; and
* identify interventions that are specific to enabling a green city to develop and evolve. Figure 3.4.2 shows a matrix that helps identify these crosscutting and integrating features. The terms of reference should clearly set out specific requirements for green city development, relating this to both sectors and themes.

Green City Integration Matrix

The matrix can be used as a base as the questions posed along the top can be modified but highlight many of the main points to be considered. By completing this matrix, it is possible to identify gaps and areas of convergence—spatial, sector, institutional. Once complete, analysis of the identified priorities against the identified long-term city development objectives and how proposed interventions support multisector and green development outcomes can take place.

Implementation

Step 3 is relevant to implementation as it identifies specialized studies or actions that may be required before additional work can commence. Such studies may include preparing greenhouse gas inventories or flood modeling. These specialized studies may take the form of a stand-alone project or may form a component of a larger project. In both instances, consideration to capacity building and specialist knowledge transfer needs to be incorporated into project design. This tool kit does not address implementation directly, but Chapter 4 includes a range of sector- and issue-specific tools that can be used during implementation.

Evaluation

Step 3 is also applied during the evaluation stage of the project cycle; it provides the feedback link to Step 1.

Under Step 3, existing projects and programs can be assessed against stated objectives and monitoring frameworks such as DMF, which helps determine impact alignment and value for money. This process will enable emerging issues to be identified and will form the basis analysis under Step 1.

Figure 3.14: Green City Integration Matrix

Sector	Green City Integrative Considerations										
	What is the spatial extent? (City level neighbourhood individual cite)	What sectors are involved?	Does it involved basic environmental infrastructure?	What planning or investment plans exit?	What landscape level or network level issues are covered?	What baseline data exits?	What Identified gap(s) is being addressed?	How has cross-sector integration been considered?	What monitoring and evaluation frameworks exits? Are all sectors reflected? How is this considered at the city?	What options for better city level integration exits?	How will the intervention assist transition through green city stages?
Improve Existing Services											
• *Identified Priorities (Phase 2)*											
New Projects											
• *Identified Priorities (Phase 2)*											
Special Interventions											
• *Identified Priorities (Phase 2)*											

Source: Emma Lewis.

4. Inventory of Existing Resources

This chapter provides a summary of available resources and tools that can be used to develop a more detailed understanding of a particular sector or topic and as a guide for developing detailed interventions. It is not an exhaustive list and will change over time. Table 4.1 is a "quick view" of each of the five urban sectors: water, solid waste, transport, energy, and the built environment. It also includes crosscutting themes such as urban, disaster risk management, climate change adaptation, green infrastructure, and project management. This chapter identifies those resources that have been reviewed in this tool kit, when it is applicable and relevant to be employed, and includes a list of relevant reference material and websites or e-resources.

4.1   Summary Matrix of Existing Tools and Resources

Table 4.1: Green City Assessment Tool Kit Overview/Resource Snapshot

Sector	Phase 1 (Preparation/Scoping) Available Tools	Phase 2 and Phase 3 (Design) Available Tools	Phase 3 (Evaluation) Available Tools
Water Sector			
Water Supply	• SWITCH: SWITCH Training Kit • Watergy • Riverlife • UNEP: Application of Sustainability Assessments of Technologies	• SWITCH: SWITCH Training Kit • Watergy • Water and Sanitation for All Tool Kit • WHO: Tools for assessing the O&M of water supply and sanitation in development countries • WSP: Guidance Notes on Services for the Urban Poor	• P. Gleick et al. A Review of Decision-Making Support Tools in the Water, Sanitation and Hygiene Sector. • WHO: Tools for assessing the O&M of water supply and sanitation in development countries
References	• Asian Development Bank. 2013. *Asian Water Development Outlook 2013: Measuring Water Security in Asia and the Pacific.* • D. Rodriguez, C. van de Berg, and A. McMahon. 2012. Investing in Water Infrastructure: Capital, Operations and Maintenance. *The paper examines major financing challenges in water infrastructure providing examples, lessons learned and outlines two tools: expenditure reviews and results-based financing.* • P. Gleick, M. Palaniappan, and M. Lang. 2008. A Review of Decision-Making Support Tools in the Water, Sanitation and Hygiene Sector. *Each chapter provides an additional related reading list.* • World Bank. 2010. Eco²Cities: Ecological Cities as Economic Cities. *Adopts a sector-based approach to explain EcoCities and relationships across sectors. Publication provides annex of sector notes.*		
Wastewater and Sanitation	• SWITCH: SWITCH Training Kit • World Bank: Design decision support • Hygiene and Sanitation Software • WSP Guidance Notes • UNEP: Application of Sustainability Assessments of Technologies • Community-led Environmental Sanitation Planning: CLUES	• SWITCH: SWITCH Training Kit • World Bank: Sanitation Marketing Tool • Hygiene and Sanitation Software • Water and Sanitation for All • Community-led Environmental Sanitation Planning: CLUES	• World Bank: Sanitation Marketing Tool • World Bank: Design decision support • Community-led Environmental Sanitation Planning: CLUES

continued on next page

Table 4.1 *continued*

Sector	Phase 1 (Preparation/Scoping) Available Tools	Phase 2 and Phase 3 (Design) Available Tools	Phase 3 (Evaluation) Available Tools
References	• C. Lüthi, A. Morel, E. Tilley, and L. Ulrich. 2011. Community-led Environmental Sanitation Planning: CLUES. Complete guidelines for decision makers with 30 tools. • C. Lüthi, A. Panesar, T. Schütze, A. Norström, J. McConville, J. Parkinson, D. Saywell, and R. Ingle. 2011. Sustainable Sanitation in Cities—A Framework for Action. Sustainable Sanitation Alliance (SuSanA) & International Forum on Urbanism (IFoU), Papiroz Publishing House, The Netherlands. • P. Gleick, M. Palaniappan, and M. Lang. 2008. A Review of Decision-Making Support Tools in the Water, Sanitation and Hygiene Sector. *Each chapter provides an additional related reading list.* • WSSCC. 2010. Hygiene and Sanitation Software: An Overview of Approaches. Geneva. • World Bank. 2010. Eco² Cities: Ecological Cities as Economic Cities. *Adopts a sector-based approach to explain EcoCities and relationships across sectors. Publication provides annex of sector notes.*		
Stormwater and Drainage			
	• SWITCH: SWITCH Training Kit • CIRIA: SusDrain • CIRIA: Planning for SuDS: Making It Happen • CIRIA: Retrofitting to Manage Surface Water	• Riverlife: Subcatchment Planning • CIRIA: SusDrain • CIRIA: Planning for SuDS: Making It Happen • CIRIA: The SuDS Manual • CIRIA: Retrofitting to Manage Surface Water	• CIRIA: SusDrain
References	• Drainage for exceedance in urban drainage—good practice • Drainage of development sites—a guide		
Water Sector Useful Websites	• Water and Sanitation Program: http://www.wsp.org/ • SusDrain: http://www.susdrain.org/ • Water Supply and Sanitation Collaborative ?Council: http://www.wsscc.org/ • Sustainable Sanitation Alliance: http://www.susana.org/		
Solid Waste Management			
	• UNEP: Application of Sustainability Assessments of Technologies.	• UNEP: Developing Integrated Solid Waste Management Plan • UNEP: Waste and Climate Change • Social Assessment and Public Participation in Municipal Solid Waste Management • ESMAP: Tool for Rapid Assessment of City Energy	• UNEP: Integrated Waste Management Scorecard
References			
Useful Websites	• UNEP: Waste Management: http://www.unep.org/ietc/OurWork/WasteManagement/tabid/56239/Default.aspx • World Bank: Urban Solid Waste Management portal: http://web.worldbank.org/WBSITE/EXTERNAL/TOPICS/EXTURBANDEVELOPMENT/EXTUSWM/0,,menuPK:463847~pagePK:149018~piPK:149093~theSitePK:463841,00.html		

continued on next page

Table 4.1 *continued*

Sector	Phase 1 (Preparation/Scoping) Available Tools	Phase 2 and Phase 3 (Design) Available Tools	Phase 3 (Evaluation) Available Tools
Transport			
	• Clean Air Portal • UNEP: Application of Sustainability Assessments of Technologies.	• RACE • ESMAP: Tool for Rapid Assessment of City Energy	• RACE • ESMAP: Tool for Rapid Assessment of City Energy
References	• World Bank. 2010. Eco^2 Cities: Ecological Cities as Economic Cities. *Adopts a sector based approach to explain EcoCities and relationships across sectors. Publication provides annex of sector notes.* • D. Bongardt, F. Creutzig, H. Hüging,K. Sakamoto, S. Bakker, Gota, S and Böhler-Baedeker, S. (2013) Low-carbon Land Transport: Policy Handbook. *Practical guide for transport policy makers and planners to achieve low-carbon land transport systems.* • Asian Development Bank. 2010. Sustainable Transport Initiative Operational Plan		
Useful Website	• Energy Sector Management Assistance Program (ESMAP): https://www.esmap.org/		
Energy			
	• ICLEI: Sustainable Energy Handbook • REEEP • UNEP: Application of Sustainability Assessments of Technologies.	• ICLEI: Sustainable Energy Handbook • EFFECT • ESMAP: MACTool • ESMAP: Tool for Rapid Assessment of City Energy	• ICLEI: Sustainable Energy Handbook • UNEP: Application of Sustainability Assessments of Technologies
Reference	• World Bank. 2010. Eco^2 Cities: Ecological Cities as Economic Cities. *Adopts a sector based approach to explain EcoCities and relationships across sectors. Publication provides annex of sector notes.*		
Useful Websites	• REEEP: http://www.reeep.org/ • Clean Air Portal: http://cleanairinitiative.org/portal/index.php • Energy Sector Management Assistance Program (ESMAP): https://www.esmap.org/ • Intergovernmental Panel on Climate Change: http://www.ipcc.ch/index.htm#.UvpNbZEyF8E		
Built Environment			
	• UNEP: Application of Sustainability Assessments of Technologies.	• LEED • BREEAM • GREEN STAR • TRACE	• LEED • BREEAM • GREEN STAR
References	• BREEAM: Good Practice Guidance: Sustainable Design and Construction • S. Angel. 2012. Planet of Cities. Lincoln Institute of Land Policy. *Innovative research and examination of urban expansion and form.*		
Useful Websites	• Energy Sector Management Assistance Program (ESMAP): https://www.esmap.org/ • Intergovernmental Panel on Climate Change: http://www.ipcc.ch/index.htm#.UvpNbZEyF8E		
Urban (General)			
	• World Bank: Eco^2 Book • ICLEI: Sustainability Planning Tool Kit* • UNEP: Application of Sustainability Assessments of Technologies • UNEP: Liveable Cities	• World Bank: Eco^2 Book • UNEP: Liveable Cities	• EIU: Asian Green City Index

continued on next page

Table 4.1   *continued*

Sector	Phase 1 (Preparation/Scoping) Available Tools	Phase 2 and Phase 3 (Design) Available Tools	Phase 3 (Evaluation) Available Tools
References	• World Bank. 2010. Eco² Cities: Ecological Cities as Economic Cities. Adopts a sector based approach to explain EcoCities and relationships across sectors. Publication provides annex of sector notes. • World Bank. Eco² Guide. Supporting documentation and guidance to complement book • UNEP. 2007. Liveable Cities: The Benefits of Urban Environmental Planning. It explores various options for sustainable urban development ranging from practical tools and comprehensive policies to innovative market mechanisms. • World Bank. 2013. Planning, Connecting, and Financing Cities Now: Priorities for City Leaders. Provides policy framework and diagnostic tools to anticipate and implement strategies that enable better long term development. • UN-Habitat. 2012. Urban Planning for City Leaders. Aims to provide local leaders and decision makers with the tools to support urban planning good practice • Asian Development Bank. 2013. Investing in Resilience: Ensuring a Disaster-Resistant Future. Is a report that outlines an approach and ideas for reflection on how to ensure that the actions required to strengthen resilience are actually taken. • Asian Development Bank. 2012. Key Indicators for Asia and the Pacific 2012: Green Urbanization in Asia, special chapter. Manila. • S. Lehmann. ADD YEAR. Green Urbanism: Formulating a Series of Holistic Principles. S.A.P.I.EN.S [Online], 3.2	2010, Online since 12 October 2010, Connection on 10 October 2012. URL: http://sapiens.revues.org/1057 • J. Eichler, A. Wegener, and U. Zimmermann. 2012. Financing Local Infrastructure—Linking Local Governments and Financial Markets. Deutsche Gesellschaft für Internationale Zusammenarbeit (GIZ) GmbH		
Useful Websites	• London School of Economics: http://lsecities.net/ • The Nature Conservancy: http://www.conservationgateway.org/ConservationPractices/EcosystemServices/Pages/ecosystem-services.aspx • Smart Cities Council: http://smartcitiescouncil.com/ • Urban Land Institute: http://asia.uli.org/ • The Pacific Cities Sustainability Initiative: http://sites.asiasociety.org/PCSI/		
Urban Resilience			
References	• Asian Development Bank. 2014. Urban Climate Change Resilience: A Synopsis. • Climate Resilient Cities: A Primer. • UNISDR. 2012. How to Make Cities More Resilient. A Handbook for Local Government Leaders/ • Asian Development Bank. 2013. Investing in Resilience. Ensuring a Disaster-Resistant future. • A. K. Jha, T. W. Miner, and Z. Stanton-Geddes, eds. 2013. Building Urban Resilience: Principles, Tools, and Practice. Directions in Development. Washington, DC: World Bank		
Useful Websites	• Asian Cities Climate Change Resilience Network (ACCRN): http://www.acccrn.org/ • International Institute for Environment and Development: http://www.iied.org/ • ICLEI Resilient Cities Forum: http://resilient-cities.iclei.org/bonn2014/resilient-cities-2014-home/ • The Pacific Cities Sustainability Initiative: http://sites.asiasociety.org/PCSI/ • The United Nation Office for Disaster Risk Reduction: http://www.unisdr.org/campaign/resilientcities/ • UNHabitat: http://unhabitat.org/urban-themes/resilience-2/ • ISET: http://i-s-e-t.org/ • The Rockefeller Foundation: http://www.rockefellerfoundation.org/our-work/current-work/climate-change-resilience		

continued on next page

Table 4.1 *continued*

Sector	Phase 1 (Preparation/Scoping) Available Tools	Phase 2 and Phase 3 (Design) Available Tools	Phase 3 (Evaluation) Available Tools
Climate Change Adaptation			
	• UKCIP: Adaptation Wizard, AdOpt • World Bank: CCA Tool Kit	• UKCIP: Risk Framework • World Bank: CCA Toolkit • UKCIP: LCLIP • RACE	• UKCIP: AdaptME • World Bank: CCA Toolkit
References	• Climate Resilient Cities: A Primer. • Asian Development Bank. 2013. Investing in Resilience: Ensuring a Disaster-Resistant Future. Manila. • A. K. Jha, T. W. Miner, and Z. Stanton-Geddes, eds. 2013. *Building Urban Resilience: Principles, Tools, and Practice*. Directions in Development. Washington, DC: World Bank • B. Smith, D. Brown, and D. Dodman. 2014. Reconfiguring Urban Adaptation finance, working paper. International Institute for Environment and Development		
Useful Websites	• Intergovernmental Panel on Climate Change: http://www.ipcc.ch/index.htm#.UvpNbZEyF8E • International Institute for Environment and Development: http://www.iied.org/		
Disaster Risk Reduction/ Management			
	• World Bank: Building Resilient Communities Toolkit • World Bank: Building Urban Resilience: Principles, Tools, and Practice	• World Bank: Cities and Flooding Guide 21st Century • World Bank: Building Resilient Communities Toolkit • World Bank: Building Urban Resilience: Principles, Tools, and Practice	• World Bank: Building Resilient Communities Toolkit • World Bank: Building Urban Resilience: Principles, Tools, and Practice.
References	• Asian Development Bank. 2013. Investing in Resilience: Ensuring a Disaster-Resistant Future. Manila. • A. K. Jha, T. W. Miner, and Z. Stanton-Geddes, eds. 2013. *Building Urban Resilience: Principles, Tools, and Practice*. Directions in Development. Washington, DC: World Bank • S. Reed, R. Friend, V. Toan, P. Thinphanga, R. Sutarto, and D. Singh. 2013) "Shared learning" for building urban climate resilience—experiences from Asian cities • D. Dodman, D. Brown, K. Francis, J. Hardoy, C. Johson, and D. Satterwaite. D., (2013) Understanding the nature and scale of urban risk in low-and middle-income countries and its implications for humanitarian preparedness, planning and response. • ISTEI: Understanding the Economics of Flood Risk Reduction • Global Assessment Report on Disaster Risk Reduction • ISDR: Indigenous Knowledge for Disaster Risk Reduction: Good Practices and Lessons Learned from Experiences in the Asia-Pacific Region		
Useful Websites	• World Bank, Disaster Risk Management East Asia & Pacific: http://web.worldbank.org/WBSITE/EXTERNAL/COUNTRIES/EASTASIAPACIFICEXT/EXTEAPREGTOPRISKMGMT/0,,menuPK:4078302~pagePK:34004175~piPK:34004435~theSitePK:4077908,00.html • UNEP: http://www.unep.org/disastersandconflicts/Introduction/DisasterRiskReduction/UNEPandDisasterRiskReduction/tabid/54353/Default.aspx • International Network for Education in Emergencies: http://www.ineesite.org/en/ • Asian Disaster Preparedness Centre: http://www.adpc.net/2012/ • International Institute for Environment and Development: http://www.iied.org/ • Prevention Web: http://www.preventionweb.net/english/hyogo/hfa-monitoring/ • Global Facility for Disaster Reduction and Recovery: https://www.gfdrr.org/		

continued on next page

Table 4.1 *continued*

Sector	Phase 1 (Preparation/Scoping) Available Tools	Phase 2 and Phase 3 (Design) Available Tools	Phase 3 (Evaluation) Available Tools
Green Infrastructure			
References	• Natural England. 2013. Green Infrastructure—Valuation Tools Assessment. • S. Naumann, M. Davis, T. Kaphengst, M. Pieterse, and M. Rayment (2011): Design, implementation and cost elements of Green Infrastructure projects. Final report to the European Commission, DG Environment, Contract no. 070307/2010/577182/ETU/F.1, Ecologic institute and GHK Consulting • B. Madsen, N. Carroll, D. Kandy, and G. Bennett. 2011. Update: State of Biodiversity Markets. Washington, DC: Forest Trends, 2011. • B. Madsen, N. Carroll, K. Moore Brands. 2010. State of Biodiversity Markets Report: Offset and Compensation Programs Worldwide.		
Useful Websites	• Ecosystems Knowledge Network: http://ecosystemsknowledge.net/ • International Institute for Environment and Development: http://www.iied.org/		
Project Management	**All stages**		
	• CDIA: City Infrastructure Investment Programming & Prioritisation Toolkit: http://www.cdia.asia/knowledge-materials/ciipp-toolkit/ • Logframes/DMFs: • Asian Development Bank: http://www.adb.org/documents/guidelines-preparing-design-and-monitoring-framework • Overseas Development Institute:; http://www.odi.org.uk/publications/5258-problem-tree-analysis • UK Government: https://www.gov.uk/government/uploads/system/uploads/attachment_data/file/67638/how-to-guid-rev-log-fmwk.pdf • Department for International Development of the United Kingdom: www.dfid.gov.uk/.../gpaf-comm-part-wdow-intro-logframes.ppt • Global Partnership Output-Based Aid: https://www.gpoba.org/node/1		

*Available only for use by members of the International Council for Local Environmental Initiatives (ICLEI—Local Governments for Sustainability).

4.2   Water Sector

SWITCH Tool

Tool: SWITCH Training Kit	Integrated Urban Water Management in the City of the Future

Objectives

To provide users with a comprehensive understanding of Integrated Urban Water Management (IUWM).

Approach

A six-module training kit that introduces users to the key concepts of IUWM and provides step-by-step guide on how to research, prepare, and implement IUWM in cities.

The tool kit is aimed at both technical staff and decision makers in local government and can be used in workshop environment or as individual reading.

The six modules are as follows:

1. Strategic Planning: Planning for the Future
2. Stakeholders: Involving all the Stakeholders
3. Water Supply: Exploring the Options
4. Stormwater: Exploring the Options
5. Wastewater: Exploring the Options
6. Decision-support Tools: Choosing a Sustainable Path

The training modules provide a summary assessment of IUWM practices against conventional practices.

Steps

The training kit has been designed to be read as a whole (all six modules) or as stand-alone individual modules. It provides the following:

- Steps for Strategic Planning (Baseline Assessment, Visioning, objectives, targets and indicators, Scenario building and development of strategy and action plan, Implementation, Monitoring and evaluation)
- Steps for Stakeholders
- Water Supply: Exploring the Options (Demand vs. Supply assessment)

The overall SWITCH approach to IUWM

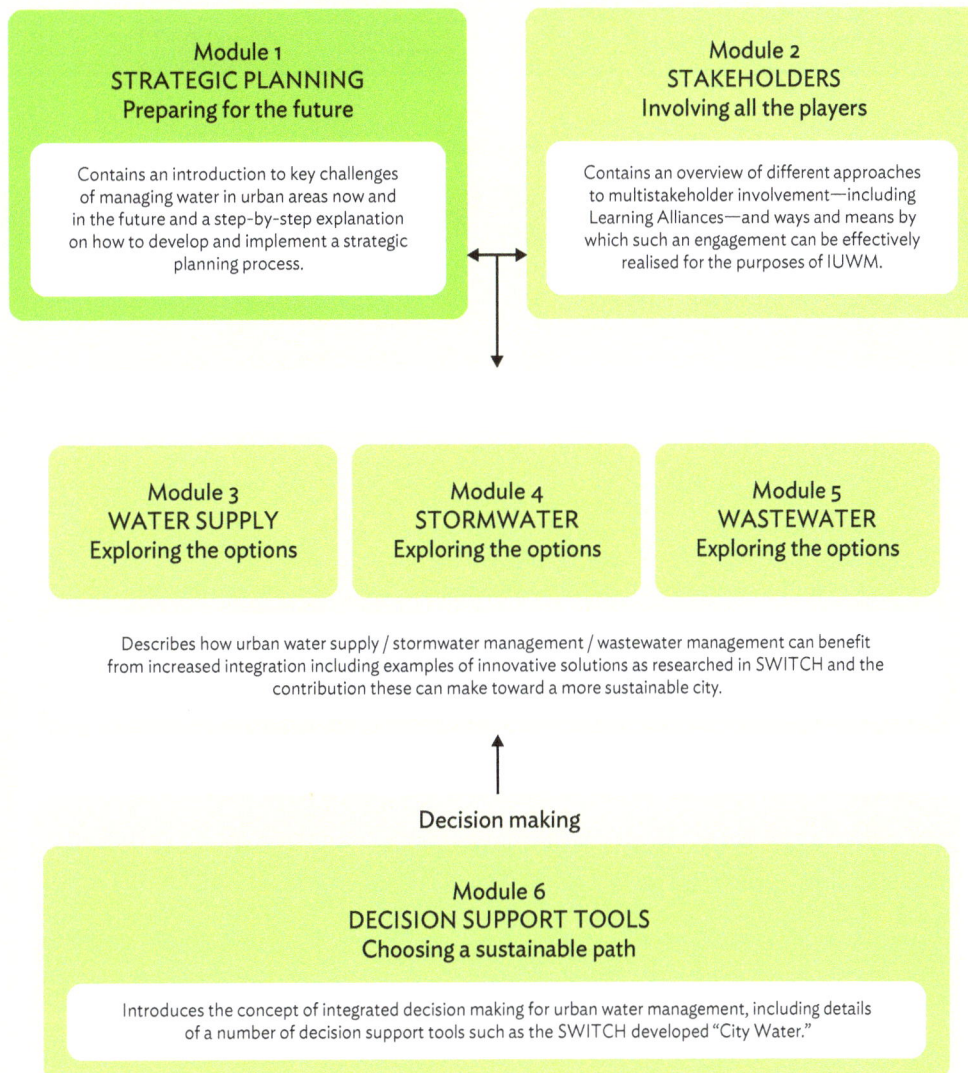

Module 1
STRATEGIC PLANNING
Preparing for the future

Contains an introduction to key challenges of managing water in urban areas now and in the future and a step-by-step explanation on how to develop and implement a strategic planning process.

Module 2
STAKEHOLDERS
Involving all the players

Contains an overview of different approaches to multistakeholder involvement—including Learning Alliances—and ways and means by which such an engagement can be effectively realised for the purposes of IUWM.

Module 3
WATER SUPPLY
Exploring the options

Module 4
STORMWATER
Exploring the options

Module 5
WASTEWATER
Exploring the options

Describes how urban water supply / stormwater management / wastewater management can benefit from increased integration including examples of innovative solutions as researched in SWITCH and the contribution these can make toward a more sustainable city.

Decision making

Module 6
DECISION SUPPORT TOOLS
Choosing a sustainable path

Introduces the concept of integrated decision making for urban water management, including details of a number of decision support tools such as the SWITCH developed "City Water."

Tool: SWITCH Training Kit	Integrated Urban Water Management in the City of the Future

Expected Results

Understanding of

- Interactions between different elements of the urban water cycle
- Wide-reaching benefits of integrated approach to managing water
- Recommended phases of strategic planning process
- Ways and means to work with local stakeholders

Identification and prioritization of water sector investment options that support IUWM.

Resources	Sustainability
Access to the tool kit is at no cost. Baseline studies required to support the strategic planning process will require funding.	IUWM adopts a systems-based approach to urban development. IUWM is a framework that enables cities to consider the water sector at all stages of the development process thus increasing sustainability.

Pointers for Implementation

The tool kit will help identify key water sector issues as well as sustainable solutions. It will provide support across all three phases of undertaking a green city assessment.

References

The SWITCH Tool Kit can be accessed here: http://www.switchtraining.eu/

Examples

Each module provides worked examples of the concept in practice.

Watergy Tool Kit

Tool: Watergy Tool Kit	Web-based tool

Objectives

Drawing on the experience of municipal water utilities around the world, the tool kit highlights innovative ways by which water utilities are reducing their energy use and, at the same time, highlights those that need to increase and improve service. Information contained within the tool kit outlines the relationship between water and energy.

By linking the management of water and energy resources, water utilities have the potential to increase energy efficiency in water supply systems. The potential benefits to individuals around the world from improving the management of water and energy resources range from cleaner air to improved economic opportunity to better utility service at lower costs.

Approach

Watergy works across both supply- and demand-side efficiency measures. The Watergy Tool Kit website provides an online resource that provides information (structured by theme) that will assist relevant agencies in improving water and energy efficiency. It considers both policy and governance issues as well as practical hardware or infrastructure requirements such as piping and pumping equipment.

Combined water and energy activities in the water supply management

Supply-side efficiency measures	**Demand-side efficiency measures** *Consumers Residential/Industrial*	**Comprehensive demand / supply side approach synergies**

Watergy efficiency is cost-effective delivery of water services, while minimizing water and energy use.

Water supply systems offer multiple opportunities to reduce water and energy waste directly, while serving customer needs more effectively.

Reducing demand by helping the consumer use water more efficiently decreases the required water supply, saving both energy and water.

Looking at a water system comprehensively and ensuring thay efficiency projects are designed in tandem create greater efficiency opportunities.

- Leak and loss reduction
- Operations and maintenance
- Pumping systems
- Primary and secondary wastewater treatment

- Water-efficient household appliances
- Low-flow toilets
- Low-flow showerheads
- Industrial water reuse
- Leak and water waste reduction

- Right-sizing pump systems after reducing consumer demand
- Avoiding wastewater treatment by promoting and reducing demand

Source: Alliance to Save Energy. 2002.

Steps

The following is from the Watergy Tool Kit and sets out the available resources:

- **Water and Energy Audits:** Through water audits and implementation assistance, a water utility can work with residential and commercial water users to improve watergy efficiency. In many cases, water audits can direct the end user to the greatest savings opportunities and act as a catalyst to induce implementation of efficiency measures. Water audits can also help bigger water customers, such as large farms, manufacturing facilities, building complexes, and universities, institute their own water management programs.
- **Leak and Loss Reduction:** In a developing country, system water losses in municipal water systems typically range from 30%to 60%; such losses stem from leakage, theft, waste, faulty equipment, and inefficient delivery. All of these factors directly affect the amount of energy required to deliver water to the consumer. An aggressive loss reduction program saves water while also reducing energy consumed by pumps, motors, and other treatment equipment.

Tool: Watergy Tool Kit   Web-based tool

- **Water Distribution System Optimization:** In order to optimize water utilities, operators must ask several questions about the distribution system: Is the system logically and efficiently designed? Does the system design take advantage of gravity? Are all parts in working order? Is water loss minimized by finding and fixing all the leaks in the distribution system? By taking a critical look at the distribution, operators can determine which short- and long-term measures need to be put in place in order to reach optimization.
- **Demand Reduction and Conservation:** Water utilities often overlook the potential of saving energy and money by reducing the water consumption of their customers. Helping customers do more with less water, using technologies such as low-flush toilets, low-flow showerheads, and energy-efficient washing machines, is often the most cost-effective way to save energy. In some instances, reducing the consumer's demand for water may allow for reductions in the capacity needs of pumps and pipes.
- **Pumps and Motors:** Pumping systems represent the highest energy demand within a municipal water utility, and offer one of the most direct opportunities for reducing energy use in a utility. Pumping system efficiency options include highly efficient pumps, variable speed drives, optimization of pump dispatching, proper pipe sizing reducing frictional losses, and proper pump sizing to match system head requirements.
- **Operations and Maintenance Practices:** Operations and maintenance cover a broad range of tasks, including equipment maintenance, pump dispatching, metering, and monitoring systems, in order to integrate efficiency into the overall water system. Simple actions, such as installing metering and monitoring systems, can pinpoint energy and water waste, often leading to a 10% reduction of energy costs simply through operational changes and improved maintenance.
- **Wastewater Treatment:** Implementing energy efficiency measures in wastewater treatment plants is important, as wastewater treatment often accounts for 25%–50% of a plant's operating budget. Some processes consume more energy than others and should receive more concentrated attention.
- **Glossary:** Comprehensive listing of the common terms used related to Water and Energy Management
- **Links:** Compilation of useful links to other organizations and resources for Watergy Managers

Expected Results

- Improved efficiency and integration across water and energy sectors
- Practical solutions to improve operations and management practice

Resources

- Tool Kit is available free of charge
- Technical expertise required for network/system design, audits, and developing response strategies
- Broad principles and technical support available for nonspecialists and can be incorporated at policy/concept stage.

Sustainability

- Considers both supply- and demand-side issues
- Adopts a cross-sector approach

Pointers for Implementation

- This tool kit identifies some of the main considerations for the water sector and its relationship to the energy sector. It can be used as a tool to assist in scoping exercises and identification of issues requiring further consideration and/or to be addressed.
- It provides a practical foundation to develop cross-sector projects/programs.

References

The tool kit and Watergy information can be accessed here: http://www.watergymex.org/Watergy%20Toolkit/resourceshttp://www.watergy.org/resources/publications/watergy.pdf

Examples

See website.

Riverlife

Tool: Subcatchment planning for sustainable water management	Riverlife

Objectives

These Guidelines provide local government with a model for

- developing sustainable water management strategies,
- improving in-house management of water and other sustainability issues,
- creating a collaborative planning environment,
- managing and understanding the complexity of urban issues, and
- finding relevant solutions to urban sustainability issues.

Approach

These guidelines provide ways to help users design an easy-to-adopt, sustainable urban water management strategy with a subcatchment focus, describing the actions to take and the reasons for doing so at each step. The guidelines show how to identify and define stormwater management priorities, collaborate with the community to create a plan, and finally implement the solutions identified through the planning process. The steps are adaptable so that management strategies for each subcatchment or other planning area can be based on the physical and social characteristics of the area, including competing land use requirements and community needs.

Steps

The guidelines set out a 10-step approach for developing and implementing sustainable urban water management practices.

1. Establishing in-house commitment to the sustainable water planning process
2. Review project budget and organizational capacity
3. Assembling a multidisciplinary team
4. Identifying physical planning units
5. Context mapping
6. Social profiling, Organizational profiling, Physical profiling
7. Determining a water budget
8. Engaging the community in sustainable water planning
9. Ways to engage the community, Creating a community water vision, Community planning forum
10. Preparing the Subcatchment Management Plans
11. Implementing the solutions
12. Communicating milestones, achievements, and outcomes

Expected Results

- Moving away from traditional water management system to an improved one.
- Sustainable water management

Resources

- Guidelines are available free of charge.
- Small multidisciplinary team for implementing/undertaking each step

Sustainability

- Rainwater harvesting
- Managing water resources as a whole
- Promoting energy-efficient products
- Approach is replicable and scalable.

Pointers for Implementation

The guidelines have been established within an Australian local government context; however, the principles and steps are applicable in Asia. Depending on the city, it may be necessary to adapt some of the governance and consultation mechanisms to reflect the situation. For example, establishing an in-house committee may require support across multiple government levels. As such, mapping the institutional arrangements first will help identify where further support is needed and what the most effective avenues for engagement are.

Reference

The guidelines can be accessed here: http://www.waterforliveability.org.au/wp-content/uploads/IUWM-Planning-Guidelines-Marrickville.pdf

Examples

Each chapter includes case study examples and a series of key points and lessons learned.

WHO: Assessing operation and maintenance status of water supply and sanitation

Tool: Tools for Assessing the O&M status of water supply and sanitation in developing Countries	World Health Organization

Objectives

Poor operation and maintenance (O&M) of water supply and sanitation constrains the sustainability of these services. This tool kit provides a framework for management and tools assessing the status of O&M through measurement and evaluation of performance. Supported by nine tools, the tool kit is targeted at policy makers who need to optimize investments in water and sanitation and professional staff (including local government employees) who are involved in the development of programs to improve actual O&M of water supply and sanitation facilities.

Approach

The nine tools are intended to measure and evaluate the effectiveness of O&M of water supply and sanitation services. Performance is measured using indicators to assess the status of O&M and to highlight successes and failures.

Prior to the detailed explanation of each individual tool, the tool kit

- explains the relevance of performance monitoring and evaluation of O&M,
- outlines different management systems for O&M and how this influences the assessment of O&M performance, and
- outlines constraints as a result of poor and/or ineffective management.

Steps

The nine tools include

Tool 1: Effectiveness of the O&M management system

Tool 2: Guidelines for an audit of O&M system

Tool 3: A framework for assessing the status of O&M

Tool 4: Guidelines on O&M performance evaluation

Tool 5: Guidelines on O&M performance reporting

Tool 6: Guidelines for selection of performance indicators

Tool 7: Performance indicators for water supply and sanitation

Tool 8: Potential information sources

Tool 9: Participatory information gathering

Expected Results

The tools will assist policy makers and professionals in

- establishing management objectives for O&M performance;
- developing a framework for performance measurement, including systems for reporting;
- carrying out measurement and reporting of performance;
- preparing action plans to improve performance;
- implementing action plans;
- continuous monitoring and reporting on performance; and
- updating and implementing the revised action plan.

Resources

- Publicly available reference document aimed at government and professional-level staff working in the water and sanitation sector and not reliant on heavy data processing
- Data collection required

Sustainability

Improving O&M enables better and more efficient services to be provided. Having basic urban environmental infrastructure in place is a fundamental building block for green cities to develop.

Pointers for Implementation

At the conclusion of each "tool" chapter, a summary of required actions is provided followed by a summary of additional reference materials. This approach enables readers to readily scope project requirements— supporting Phase 1 and Phase 2 of the green city assessment process well.

Reference

The document can be accessed here: http://www.who.int/water_sanitation_health/hygiene/om/omtools/en/

Examples

Worked examples are not provided; however, detailed guidance and summary boxes highlighting key concepts and considerations are provided.

Decision-Making Support Tools

Tool: A review of decision-making support tools in the water, sanitation, and hygiene sector.   **Pacific Institute and the Environmental Change and Security Program (ECSP)**

Objectives

Water, Sanitation and Hygiene (WASH) challenges continue to be a major barrier to development, affecting health, mortality, and productivity particularly in developing countries. This document aims to inform the preparation of a new decision-support tool for the WASH sector that responds to the analysis undertaken of existing tools and serves to provide practitioners with the best options to meet WASH requirements. It provides an overview of existing resources, identifying gaps and providing a conceptual framework to address these.

Approach

Effectively addressing community needs requires that technologies or approaches be economically, ecologically, and socially appropriate and sustainable. Consideration of the WASH sector occurs at geographic scale (area affected/covered) and topic (expanded below):

- Technological comparison—Inclusion of descriptions, figures, tables, lists, or other mechanisms that compare the benefits and disadvantages of technologies in a side-by-side manner.
- Construction—Information on how to build or implement water and sanitation infrastructure and technologies.
- Operation and maintenance (O&M)—Information on the specific O&M requirements for a technology, or a general discussion of O&M within a framework or methodology.
- Community involvement—Information on the role of the community or community members in water and sanitation projects, specifically their role in planning, implementation, evaluation, or O&M; and information on a specific technology/method/approach that relies on community involvement.
- Institutional aspects—Information on the role that government bodies, community groups, banks, businesses, and others play in the planning, implementation, promotion, construction, evaluation, or maintenance of water and sanitation-related method or technology.
- Cost of technologies—Information on water and sanitation infrastructure construction and O&M costs, the price consumers and providers pay for water and sanitation services using specific technologies or systems, and any other incurred costs.
- Financing—Discussion of approaches to financing specific water and sanitation technologies or general projects.
- Evaluation and monitoring—Information on the evaluation and/or monitoring of water and sanitation improvement projects in general, or with respect to projects that use specific technologies or systems.
- Scalability and replicability—Information on or discussion of how well particular technologies or approaches are suited to being replicated in other regions, or how easy it is to scale up a particular approach to larger geographic areas.

Steps

- Design of a Decision-Making Support Tool: This would incorporate all the elements to control morbidity and mortality from the water supply system and thus addressing interconnected factors such as water supply, drinking water treatment, sanitation, wastewater treatment, and hygiene.
- Dissemination of a Decision-Making Support Tool: This is to be done through regional workshops and works of technical support team.

Expected Results

- Improved and easy access to water-sanitation infrastructure/facilities
- Sustainability and effectiveness in service delivery through constant monitoring and evaluation
- Fulfilling the community needs through effective community involvement.

Resources	Sustainability
In the WASH field, evaluation tools tend to focus on sources of drinking water, technologies for drinking water treatment, household sanitation technologies, and wastewater treatment.	Improved decision making through structured and regular monitoring and evaluation of performance, effectiveness, and value for money.

Pointers for Implementation

- While strictly speaking not a tool that assists users in preparing an output, Chapters 3 and 4 provide a useful summary of gaps in existing decision-making support tools. This is followed by a conceptual framework for a new tool to be developed. These two chapters are particularly useful for Phase 1 and Phase 2 of the city assessment to develop an intervention that addresses these issues.
- Appendix A provides a bibliography of relevant resources.
- Appendix B provides a detailed summary, including bibliography.

Reference

The document can be accessed here: http://www.pacinst.org/reports/WASH_tool/WASH_decisionmaking_tools.pdf

Example

Conceptual framework for new tool provided.

Practical Guide for Improving Water Supply

Tool: Water and Sanitation Program: Guidance notes on services for the urban poor	A practical guide for improving water supply and sanitation services

Objectives

The guidance note targets project planners, services providers, and community leaders to enable them to identify the barriers to providing adequate services to the urban poor. The guidance note aims to provide practical actions that can primarily be implemented within existing frameworks.

Approach

The guidance note provides a systematic analysis of the barriers to service delivery for the urban poor and provides practical solutions and strategies to overcome these barriers. Structured in eight chapters, each introduces the issue and the main challenges, and sets out the required actions to improve water supply and sanitation. These actions are supported by information on required resources. The document can be read as a whole or as stand-alone individual chapters.

Strong emphasis is placed on participatory planning and engagement that is supported with practical options to improve service provision. The focus is on results-based intervention operating within existing frameworks rather than promotion of policy reform.

Each chapter concludes with a series of case studies and further reading or additional resources list.

Steps

The guidance note provides a "how to" and required resources in the following areas:

- Giving the poor a voice
- Build support for improving services
- Eliminate administrative and legal barriers
- Strengthen capacity, autonomy, and accountability of service providers and provide incentives to serve the poor
- Adopt appropriate investment finance, cost recovery, and subsidy policies
- Overcome physical and technical barriers
- Includes a section on alternative technologies and delivery systems
- Modular planning

Expected Results

- Design inclusive water supply and sanitation initiatives
- Understand the benefit of working as far as practicable within existing frameworks
- Understanding of alternative technologies
- Incorporation of modular planning within strategic planning

Resources

- Aimed at policy and decision makers, and is publicly available. Resources are staff/government time preparing documents and undertaking community consultation/engagement exercises.

Sustainability

- Explains and encourages modular planning as system components are initially designed with limited excess capacity as a means of reducing initial investment costs.
- Supports inclusive development and provision of services to the urban poor.

Pointers for Implementation

At the conclusion of each chapter, a "getting started" section has been prepared, clearly setting out the required resources, objectives, and expected outcomes of each step.

Reference

The document can be accessed here: http://www.wsp.org/sites/wsp.org/files/publications/Main_Global_Guidance_Note.pdf

Examples

Case study examples covering Brazil, India, Pakistan, the Philippines, Tanzania, and Zambia are provided.

4.3   Sanitation

Hygiene and Sanitation Software

Tool: Hygiene and Sanitation Software	Water Supply and Sanitation Collaborative Council (WSSCC)

Objectives

To provide an overview of the various hygiene and sanitation "software" approaches developed over the last 40 years. Based on this overview, to provide a concise reference document of commonly used approaches within the hygiene and sanitation sector.

The interventions aim to

- empower individuals, schools, and/or communities with knowledge;
- enable a change in behavior;
- create demand for services;
- facilitate establishment of supply chains; or
- improve the planning and implementation of hygiene and sanitation projects.

Approach

The tool focuses on four main areas:

- Participatory Planning Tools
- Behavior Change and Hygiene Promotion
- Creating Demand and Supply Chains
- Programming Frameworks

Each main topic area is then examined and an analysis of available tools is undertaken. The analysis is presented in color-coded summary table that outlines

- Tool goal,
- Target audience/group,
- Application details,
- Description of tool and outline of best use and appropriate use (using the Hygiene and Sanitation ladders),
- Assessment of strengths and weaknesses,
- Summary of evidence of effectiveness, and
- Sources of information and additional resources.

Hygiene and Sanitation Ladder

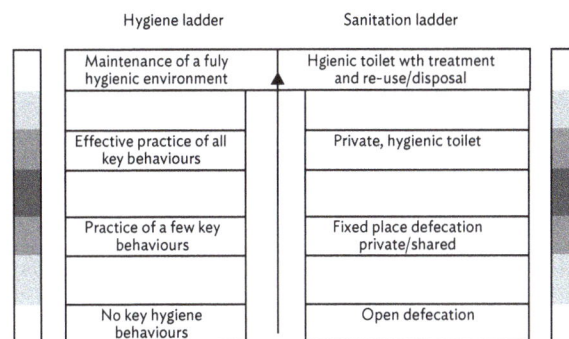

Hygiene ladder	Sanitation ladder
Maintenance of a fuly hygienic environment	Hgienic toilet wth treatment and re-use/disposal
Effective practice of all key behaviours	Private, hygienic toilet
Practice of a few key behaviours	Fixed place defecation private/shared
No key hygiene behaviours	Open defecation

Steps

The structure and focus of the tool kit in the four topic areas allow users to access the most relevant information based on individual circumstance. The list below summarizes the tools and information available under each topic.

- Participatory Planning Tools
  Self-esteem, Associated strengths, Resourcefulness, Action planning, Responsibility (SARAR)
  Methodology for Participatory Assessments (MPA)
  Community Action Planning
- Behavior Change and Hygiene Promotion
  Participatory, Community-Based "total" Hygiene
  Marketing and Single Intervention
- Creating Demand and Supply Chains
  Community-wide Approaches
  Marketing of Sanitation Goods and Services
- Programming Frameworks

Tool: Hygiene and Sanitation Software	Water Supply and Sanitation Collaborative Council (WSSCC)

Expected Results

- Identification of most appropriate interventions based on evidence presented and project city context
- Improved understanding of key issues and barriers to behavior change
- Improved understanding of the role of software interventions and the relationship between software and hardware interventions

Resources	**Sustainability**
• Minimal resources required, time of relevant staff or user to read document • Design of intervention based on tool kit will vary depending on task. • Implementation of proposed responses will require additional resources.	• Behavior change and increased knowledge within the community in relation to sanitation and hygiene can be integrated with key messages for green cities. This is important and includes the role of individuals improving the urban environment. • Software interventions must be considered in conjunction with hardware interventions, and this can include crosscutting topics such as green infrastructure and watershed management and health.

Pointers for Implementation

This tool is most useful during Phase 1 of the green city assessment as it helps to improve knowledge on current software approaches within the sanitation and hygiene sector. The summary table, which provides an analysis of strengths and weaknesses of individual tools, is particularly useful when considering the design of new projects.

Reference

The document can be accessed here: http://www.wsscc.org/sites/default/files/publications/wsscc_hygiene_and_sanitation_software_2010.pdf

Examples

See Part 3 of resource for detailed case study examples covering Bangladesh, Benin, Ethiopia, and India.

Community-Led Urban Environmental Sanitation

Tool: Community-Led Urban Environmental Sanitation: Complete guidelines for decision makers with 30 tools	Eawag–Sandec, WSSCC, UN-Habitat

Objectives

To enable urban communities and municipalities in low-income countries to plan and implement cost-effective environmental sanitation services that employ appropriate technologies suited to user needs.

Approach

- Community-Led Urban Environmental Sanitation (CLUES) promotes a shift away from centralized conventional sewerage (but does not exclude it) toward offering a range of technology solutions for people living in poor and unplanned urban areas. The reference guide details a seven-step approach (see Figure 4.17) and identifies three crosscutting tasks:
- Awareness Raising and Communication
- Capacity Development
- Process Monitoring and Evaluation

Steps

- The reference guide sets out in detail the seven-step approach, and a summary is provided in the figure below:

Figure 4.17 : The Seven-Step CLUES approach

Overview of the CLUES planning approach

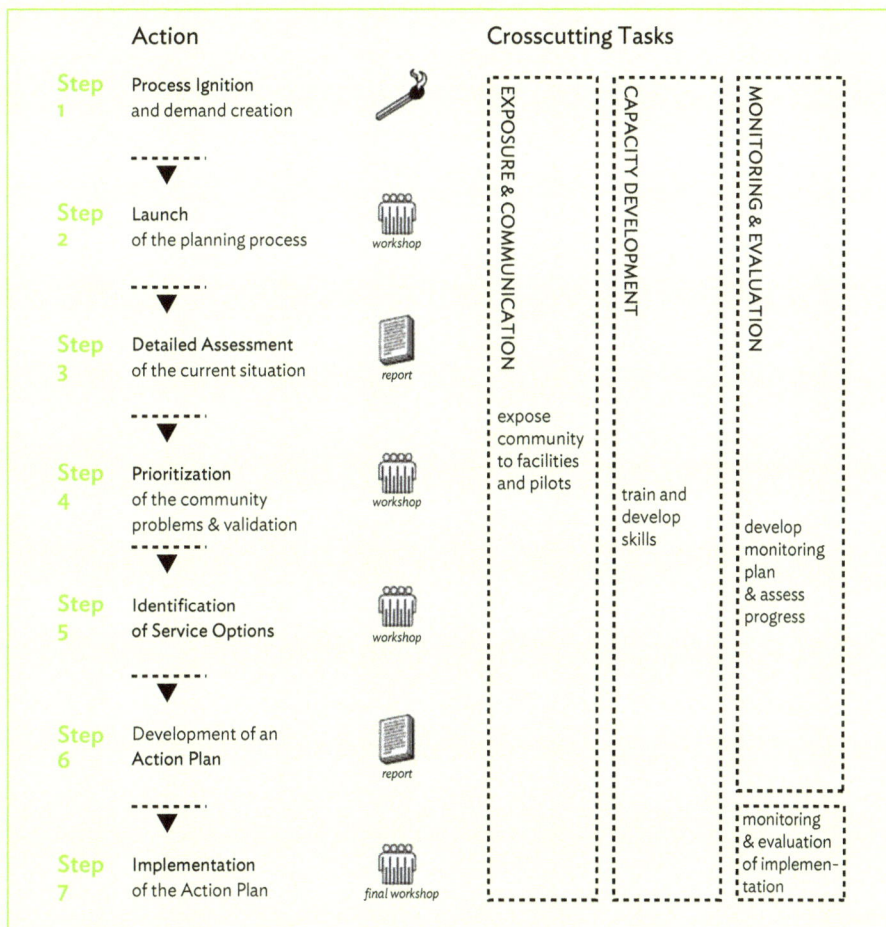

CLUES = Community-Led Urban Environmental Sanitation.

Source: http://www.susana.org/en/resources/library/details/1300

Tool: Community-Led Urban Environmental Sanitation: Complete guidelines for decision makers with 30 tools	Eawag–Sandec, WSSCC, UN-Habitat

Expected Results

- Identification of most appropriate interventions based on evidence presented and project city context
- Improved understanding of key issues and barriers to behavior change
- Improved understanding of the role of software interventions and the relationship between software and hardware interventions

Resources	Sustainability
<ul><li>The budget estimated by the authors of the book to undertake steps 1–6 is $15,000.</li><li>Time of staff and practitioners to access and read document</li><li>Design of intervention based on tool kit will vary depending on task.</li><li>Implementation of proposed responses will require additional resources.</li></ul>	<ul><li>Behavior change and increased knowledge within the community in relation to sanitation and hygiene can be integrated with key messages for green cities. This is important and includes the role of individuals improving the urban environment.</li><li>Integrated and community-led planning initiatives.</li></ul>

Pointers for Implementation

The reference guide includes a practical and useful description of an "enabling environment" (Part 2 of the guide). This section is relevant to green city development as it enables wider and more strategic issues to be identified and considered. Consider these issues when completing the needs assessment matrix to identify relevant crosscutting issues and areas for intervention.

Part 2 also provides a useful guide for undertaking institutional assessments.

Part 3 includes a detailed summary of 30 available tools and related to the seven-step process.

Reference

The document can be accessed here: http://www.susana.org/docs_ccbk/susana_download/2-1300-cluesguid.pdf

Examples

Each section of Parts 1 and 2 of the book concludes with a summary of a practice example of the principle/approached explained.

Marketing Tool

Tool: Sanitation Marketing Tool	Water and Sanitation Program

Objectives

To introduce an emerging field of practice "sanitation marketing," which looks to improve sanitation through behavior change encouraged by active engagement and education strategies

Approach

The tool considers the "sanitation challenge" and how "sanitation marketing" can support the challenge. Sanitation challenge refers to the large number of people worldwide who lack access to improved sanitation. Sanitation marketing has been framed within the context of "social marketing"—a process for creating, communicating, and delivering benefits that a target population desires in exchange for adopting a behavior that profits society (Kotler and Lee, as cited in Devine and Kullmann). Supporting this are the marketing 4Ps (product, place, price, promotion) and how this can be used effectively for sanitation promotion.

The main component of the tool is SaniFOAM, which categorizes the behavioral factors for sanitation under three headings—Opportunity, Ability, and Motivation—and broadly defined as

Opportunity: Does the individual have the chance to perform the behavior? Determinants under this category include access and availability (e.g., proximity to a local retailer), product attributes (e.g., ease of cleaning), social norms (e.g., acceptability of open defecation), and sanctions/enforcement (e.g., fines for open defecation).

Ability: Is the individual capable of performing it? Determinants under this category include knowledge (e.g., awareness of the causes of diarrhea), skills and self-efficacy (e.g., ability to dig a pit),social support (e.g., willingness to share one's latrine with a neighbor), roles and decisions (e.g., who in the household manages the budget), and affordability (e.g., cash available).

Motivation: Does the individual want to perform it? Determinants under this category include attitudes and beliefs (e.g., misconceptions about infants' excreta) and social drivers (e.g., status), physical/emotional drivers (e.g., comfort), values (e.g., modernity), competing priorities (e.g., tuition, television), intention (e.g., stage of saving for a toilet), and willingness to pay (e.g., presence of government subsidies).

Based on this research, a marketing strategy is devised and implemented.

Steps

- Define the need and purpose of the research (Need, Information)
- Define the research objectives and questions
- Development of approach and study design
- Data collection
- Assessment
- Conclusion

Expected Results

- Improved understanding of how marketing principles can be effectively applied to the sanitation sector to influence behavior change.

Resources	Sustainability
- Print and online resource available at no cost to users - Template and sample tools provided	Tool kit has been developed with a focus on rural areas. How it can be applied in an urban context is an important consideration.

Pointers for Implementation

The tool kit is available as an online training module and in printed form.

Each chapter includes a summary of key concepts and case study examples of how each principle can or has been applied.

Templates and sample questionnaires or other support and research tools are included in the tool kit.

The tool kit provides summary implementation and resource schedule.

References

The document can be accessed here: http://www.wsp.org/sites/wsp.org/files/publications/WSP-Introductory-Guide-Sanitation-Marketing.pdf

The online training module can be accessed here: http://www.wsp.org/toolkit/toolkit-home

Examples

Worked examples are provided throughout the entire document.

Practitioners Companion

**Tool: Water and Sanitation for All Tool Kit:
A Practitioner's Companion**   **Online Resource**

Objectives

The aim of the tool kit is to provide practitioners, policy makers, and decision makers information on current trends and knowledge gained from past experience regarding water supply and sanitation service delivery to low income urban areas.

The tool kit should enable readers to identify problems or challenges, and draw up a strategy for addressing these challenges using information and other resources assembled for this purpose.

Approach

The tool kit is based on information gathered over several years from a series of consultative workshops at the country and regional levels; it considers the existing resources and knowledge of sector practitioners and research carried out by various institutions.

It offers practical advice on getting to know low income customers better; presents pros and cons of a range of options for service delivery; suggests how various institutions may support improvements in service delivery; identifies key policy, legal, and regulatory features; looks into financing issues and mechanisms; and provides the reader with a wide range of resources to work with.

The tool kit has been developed and updated over time, building on experience and knowledge generated through various activities at the country, regional, and international levels. It has been developed through the Water Utility Partnership (WUP) Project No. 5—Improving Utilities Capacity to Deliver Water Supply and Sanitation Services to Low Income Urban Communities; and Project No. 4—Hygiene Education and Environmental Health.

Steps

An interactive website is structured in six main areas:

- Action Checklist
- Customers and Providers
- Policies and Legal Aspects
- Funding and Cost Recovery
- Levels of Service
- Resources

Users click on the relevant topic area tabs to be directed to the range of resources available. Each section is structured slightly differently but approaches the topic in a similar manner by introducing key issues (including key questions to ask) and followed supporting information, examples, and instructions on how to complete respective activities. Each service delivery option also includes the following:

- Description of the option
- Summary of advantages and disadvantages
- Identification and explanation of principles being addressed
- Management options, including the different types of institutional arrangements and implications of each
- Summary of potential impact and considerations of each option over short-, medium-, and long-term time horizons within the context of sustainability or suitability for extension to improve service level.
- The resources tab includes a subsection titled "Tools." This tab provides supporting tools across all topic areas and includes hyperlinks to referenced material.

Expected Results

- Improved understanding of issues and principles that guide service delivery to low-income communities
- Practical solutions to improve knowledge and understanding of low-income customers
- Identification of advantages and disadvantages of multiple service delivery options
- Identification of appropriate institutional arrangements to improve service delivery
- Identification and improved understanding of required policy, legal, and regulatory features
- Understanding of possible financing mechanisms including leveraging private sector involvement
- Awareness of available resources

Tool: Water and Sanitation for All Tool Kit: A Practitioner's Companion	Online Resource
Resources	**Sustainability**
• Publicly available tool and resource kit • Each topic area has different technical and staffing requirements. Main resource requirements will be staff to undertake assessments, prepare draft reports, and conduct community consultation.	• Adopts an integrated approach considering both supply-and demand-side issues.

Pointers for Implementation

The tool is web based and therefore each resource is available online and linked to the materials referenced. This means it is difficult to download some materials and work offline.

Reference

The tool kit can be accessed here: http://web.mit.edu/urbanupgrading/waterandsanitation/home.html

Examples

The website includes a section titled "Case Examples." Here, detailed examples of predominantly African case studies are accessible.

4.4   Stormwater Management and Drainage

Sustainable Drainage

Tool: SuDS Manual	CIRIA 2007

Objectives

To provide best practice guidance on the planning, design and construction, and operation and maintenance of Sustainable Urban Drainage Systems (SuDS) to facilitate effective implementation

Approach

Appropriately designed, constructed, and maintained SuDS provide a more sustainable alternative to conventional drainage methods as they can mitigate many of the adverse effects of urban stormwater runoff on the environment. Key benefits that can be delivered via SuDS include

• Reducing runoff rates, thus reducing downstream flooding.
• Reducing the additional runoff volumes and frequencies that tend to be increased as a result of urbanization and can exacerbate flood risk and damage receiving water quality.
• Encouraging natural groundwater recharge to minimize impacts on aquifers and river base flows in the receiving catchment.
• Reducing pollutant concentrations in stormwater.
• Reducing the volume of surface water runoff discharging into combined sewer systems, thus reducing discharges of polluted water to watercourses via Combined Sewer Overflow (CSO) spills.

Tool: SuDS Manual   CIRIA 2007

Steps

| The background: Understanding SUOS principles and process | Chapter 1: Introduction
Chapter 2: Roles, responsibilities, and regulation
Chapter 3: Design criteria |

| SuDS scheme: Feasibility | Chapter 2: Roles, responsibilities, and regulation
Chapter 3: Design criteria
Chapter 4: Design methods
Chapter 5: SuDS selection
Chapter 21: Construction
Chapters 22 & 23: Operation, maintenance, and waste
Chapter 24: Community engagement
Chapter 25: Costs and benefits |

| SuDS scheme: Detailed design | Chapter 4: Design methods
Chapters 6 & 7: Source control and pretreatment
Chapters 8–18: Individual component design details
Chapter 19: Inlet and outlet design
Chapter 20: Landscaping |

| Community engagement/risk management | Chapter 24: Community engagement |

| Operation and maintenance plan | Chapter 22: Operation and maintenance
Chapter 23: Waste management |

| Construction planning | Chapter 20: Landscaping
Chapter 21: Construction
C698: Construction handbook |

| Putting long-term funding for maintenance in place | Chapter 25: Costs and benefits |

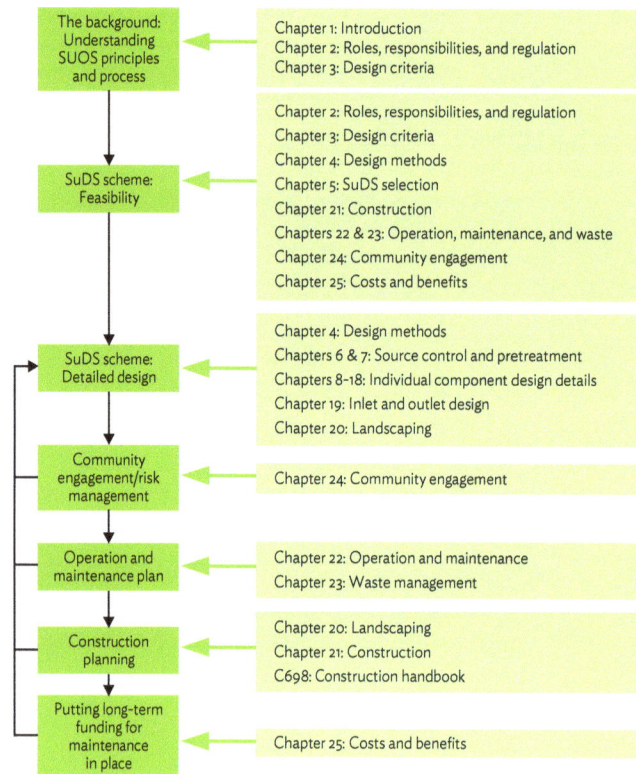

Expected Results

- SuDS integrated within strategic planning process
- Improved flood risk management
- Improved resilience
- Provision of green infrastructure—including multifunctional public open space
- Identify opportunities for retrofitting within urban areas to achieve SuDS

Resources

- CIRIA offers membership for professional staff and organizations, which includes paid subscriptions and publicly available free resources. This manual is readily available following a registration process.
- Implementing and/or designing SuDS interventions require specialist inputs from a range of disciplines.

Sustainability

- SuDS provide an opportunity to design with the flow of water and providing sufficient space for it to flow. This approach is underpinned by the objective of reducing potential negative impacts during flood events or heavy water flows. Implementing principles of SuDS improves both resilience and sustainability of areas.

Pointers for Implementation

The examples provided in this guidance document are predominantly focused on implementation in the United Kingdom. This does not detract from the utility of the document, however, as the key concepts and more importantly explanations of technical solutions are applicable across multiple contexts. Further, the methodological approach of SuDS and applying this within a strategic planning framework also stand regardless of geography. Importantly, within an Asian city context, SuDS will have a significant role when considering urban flooding and improving resilience through improved drainage systems. Integrating SuDS principles within the urban development process is a fundamental element to improve sustainability and advance the green city agenda.

Reference

The guidance can be accessed here: http://www.ciria.org

The guidance is free and available online. Prior to accessing the document, the user is required to register on the CIRIA website. The document is then readily available to be downloaded.

Examples

The document provides succinct examples, pictures, and descriptions of key concepts and approaches to SuDS.

Planning for Sustainable Drainage

Tool: Planning for SuDS—Making it Happen	CIRIA 2010

Objectives

To provide a comprehensive overview of sustainable urban drainage systems followed by a step-by-step guide on how to develop, implement, and maintain sustainable drainage systems (SuDS) in urban areas

Approach

Water is an essential part of the natural and built environment and, increasingly, as the pressure of urbanization is felt, the importance of sustainable water management becomes more pronounced. SuDS adopt a more natural approach to managing rainfall where it falls for any site. SuDS are an important part of delivering sustainable communities and development and can be considered as part of wider provision of urban services such as public open space, parking, transport, etc. that can be referred to as green infrastructure.

Sustainable drainage provides an opportunity to deliver multiple benefits within a development, and this guidance provides an introduction to key concepts, approaches (demonstrated by case studies), and a series of "how to" chapters to assist users in the design and implementation of SuDS.

Steps

The guidance is structured so as to allow users to

- Identify what SuDS options are available
- Integrate into the development and planning process
- Learn how to implement
- Know the operation and maintenance requirements

Expected Results

- SuDS integrated within strategic planning process
- Improved flood risk management
- Improved resilience
- Provision of green infrastructure—including multifunctional public open space
- Identify opportunities for retrofitting within urban areas to achieve SuDS

Resources

- CIRIA offers membership for professional staff and organizations, which includes paid subscriptions and publicly available free resources. This manual is readily available following a registration process.
- Implementing and/or designing SuDS interventions require specialist inputs from a range of disciplines.

Sustainability

- SuDS provide an opportunity to design with the flow of water and providing sufficient space for it to flow. This approach is underpinned by the objective of reducing potential negative impacts during flood events or heavy water flows. Implementing principles of SuDS improves both resilience and sustainability of areas.

Pointers for Implementation

The examples provided in this guidance document are predominantly focused on implementation in the United Kingdom. This does not detract from the utility of the document, however, as the key concepts and, more importantly, explanations of technical solutions are applicable across multiple contexts. Further, the methodological approach or SuDS and applying this within a strategic planning framework also stand regardless of geography. Importantly, within an Asian city context, SuDS will have a significant role when considering urban flooding and improving resilience through improved drainage systems. Integrating SuDS principles within the urban development process is a fundamental element to improve sustainability and advance the green city agenda.

Reference

The guidance can be accessed here: http://www.ciria.org

The guidance is free and available online. Prior to accessing the document, the user is required to register on the CIRIA website. The document is then readily available to be downloaded.

Examples

Practical examples of practice from within the United Kingdom are provided.

Retrofitting to Manage Surface Water

Tool: Retrofitting to Manage Surface Water	CIRIA 2012

Objectives

To retrofit urban areas with surface water management measures that will include drainage systems that mimic natural drainage processes; manage pollution alongside flood risk; adopt and manage extreme events; and improve biodiversity, amenity, and resilience to climate change.

Approach

This guidance note provides a framework to assist in the more effective retrofitting of surface water management measures. It sets out how to adopt a strategic or opportunistic retrofit approach.

It is divided into three parts:

Part A: Overview and introduction to key concepts surface water management measures

Part B: Main guidance—retrofitting framework

Part C: Case studies

Steps

Framework for retrofitting surface water management measures:

- Preparation
- Feasibility
- Developing options
- Appraisal
- Implementation
- Performance monitoring

Expected Results

- Improved urban drainage
- Increased resilience
- Adaptive urban spaces
- Integration with green infrastructure
- Improved urban design

Resources

The guidance is aimed at professionals working within the planning and development sector.

Sustainability

SuDS provide an opportunity to design with the flow of water and providing sufficient space for it to flow. This approach is underpinned by the objective of reducing potential negative impacts during flood events or heavy water flows. Implementing principles of SuDS improves both resilience and sustainability of areas. This guidance note supports retrofitting developed areas to achieve this.

Pointers for Implementation

The examples provided in this guidance document are predominantly focused on implementation in the United Kingdom. This does not detract from the utility of the document, however, as the key concepts and, more importantly, explanations of technical solutions are applicable across multiple contexts. Further, the methodological approach of SuDS and applying this within a strategic planning framework also stand regardless of geography. Importantly, within an Asian city context, SuDS will have a significant role when considering urban flooding and improving resilience through improved drainage systems. Integrating SuDS principles within the urban development process is a fundamental element to improve sustainability and advance the green city agenda.

Reference

The guidance can be accessed here: http://www.ciria.org

The guidance is free and available online. Prior to accessing the document, the user is required to register on the CIRIA website. The document is then readily available to be downloaded.

Examples

The document showcases 10 case studies demonstrating SuDS in practice and highlighting key concepts.

E-resources

Tool: SusDrain	Online reference

Objectives

Online resource providing information and support to sustainable urban drainage and management.

Approach

Provides a range of resources for those involved in delivering sustainable drainage systems (SuDS). SuDS help manage flood risk and water quality, and provide a range of amenity benefits that create great places to live, work, and play.

SusDrain has been created by the Construction Industry Research and Information Association (CIRIA).

Summary of Resources

SusDrain provides up-to-date guidance, information, case studies, videos, photos, and discussion forums that help underpin the planning, design, approval, construction, and maintenance of SuDS.

Expected Results

Awareness of available resources, and current and emerging good practice.

Reference

The online resource can be accessed here: http://www.susdrain.org/

Tool: World Bank: Water and Sanitation Program (WSP)	Online reference

Objectives

The Water and Sanitation Program (WSP) is a multidonor partnership administered by the World Bank to support the poor in obtaining affordable, safe, and sustainable access to water and sanitation services.

Approach

WSP works on six core topics. Each area is anchored with a focus of helping governments monitor for improved service provision to ensure sustainability, make the best use of available resources, and inform sector planning. The six core topics are as follows:

- Supporting Poor-Inclusive Water Supply and Sanitation (WSS) Sector Reform
- Targeting the Urban Poor and Improving Services in Small Towns
- Adapting WSS Delivery to Climate Change Impacts
- Creating Sustainable Services through Domestic Private Sector Participation
- Delivering WSS Services in Fragile States
- Scaling Up Rural Sanitation and Hygiene

Summary of Resources

The website is structured by geographic area and topic that is supported by an online library catalog.

Expected Results

- Awareness of available resources, and current and emerging good practice

Reference

The website can be accessed here: http://www.wsp.org/

4.5   Solid Waste Management

Application of Sustainability Assessments of Technologies

Tool: Application of Sustainability Assessments of Technologies	United Nations Environment Programme (UNEP)

Objectives

Developed by the International Environmental Technology Centre (IETC) Sustainability Assessment of Technologies (SAT) is an extension of Environmental Technology Assessment (EnTA). EnTA is a systematic procedure whereby a proposed technology intervention is described and appraised in terms of its potential influence on the environment, implications for sustainable development, and the likely cultural and socioeconomic consequences.

The SAT methodology enables a set of criteria and indicators to be developed in the following categories:

- Technological suitability,
- Environmental considerations (in terms of resources, emissions, risk, etc.),
- Economic/financial concerns, and
- Sociocultural considerations.

It provides an assessment framework that can be applied at both the strategic and operational levels to a range of sectors that include

- End-of-pipe or waste management systems,
- Environmental health programs,
- Provision of basic services and infrastructure (water, roads, power, etc.),
- Biodiversity management,
- Remediation/land reclamation,
- Process technology modernization (industrial clusters), and
- Recycling programs.

Approach

A tiered assessment applicable across all levels is set out below.

Policy and Government Level	• For strategic planning and policy making
Financing Institution Level	• For assessing projects for funding
Operational Level	• For assessment of alternative technologies
Community and Cluster Level	• For assessment and comparison of collective alternative technologies
Village/Enterprise Level	• For comparing technology options

Adopting tiered assessment (see below), the document then sets out a step-by-step guide on what is required, how to conduct each task under the various steps, and how this may be applied at each level—from strategic to operational.

It concludes with a series of training examples for users to I test by undertaking a SAT followed by completed worked exercise.

Steps

The tiered assessment includes

- Screening,
- Scoping (establishes a shortlist), and
- Detailed assessment (identifies technology systems most suitable to situation).

The Sustainability Assessment of Technologies (SAT) Methodology

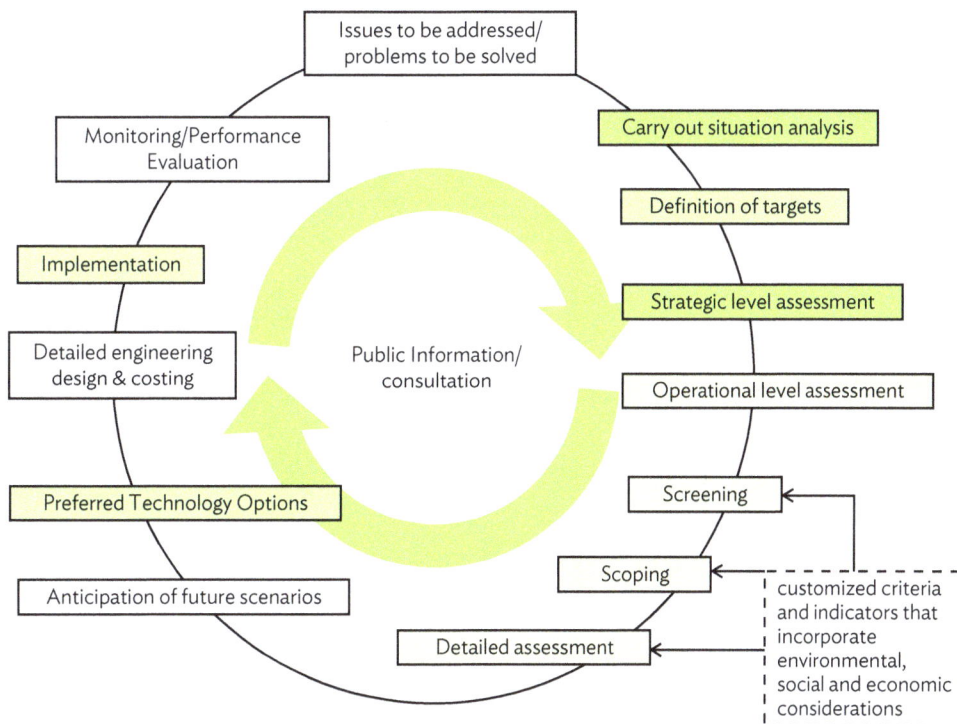

Source: United Nations Environment Programme. 2012. *Application of the Sustainability Assessment of Technologies Methodology: Guidance Manual.*

Expected Results

- Identification of most appropriate technology option that considers environmental, sociocultural, economic, and financial considerations in addition to technological suitability.

Resources

This reference is readily available online. As it is primarily a resource aimed at supporting an assessment process, the implications for users/resources are minimal. However, depending on the project, implementation, and the continued cycle of review, assessment and management does have implications for the level of resources required.

Sustainability

The applicability across multiple stages of a project enables a continued cycle of review and assessment, and thus reflects the iterative nature of urban development.

Pointers for Implementation

A case study and training tools are provided to enable the user to apply the assessment methodology. Each section is then explained in full in the following section, enabling users to learn by doing. The training section is structured with sections that highlighted "guidance" boxes. These provide useful tips and explanations of key concepts.

Reference

The document can be accessed here: http://www.unep.org/ietc/InformationResources/Publications/ SustainabilityAssessmentofTechnologyManual/tabid/106701/Default.aspx

Example

The training section provides a worked case study applying the methodology for biomass facilities in Sri Lanka.

Developing an Integrated Solid Waste Management Plan

Tool: Developing an Integrated Solid Waste Management Plan	United Nations Environment Programme (UNEP)

Objectives

To provide a comprehensive overview and guidance on how to prepare an Integrated Solid Waste Management Plan (ISWMP)

Approach

A four-volume series of guidance has been prepared to enable the preparation of an ISWMP. The four volumes include

- waste characterization and quantification,
- assessment of current waste management system,
- target issues and concerns, and
- ISWMP.

Steps

- Waste characterization and quantification: Step one focuses on the collection and analysis of data to generate baseline information on waste characterization and quantification with projections in the future. It is the first step in the preparation of an ISWMP.
- Assessment of current waste management system: Step two focuses on the collection and analysis of data to generate baseline information on current waste management system with identification of gaps therein. This second step is important to develop an ISWMP to avoid duplication or reinventing the wheel and to prioritize actions.
- Target issues and concerns: This third step is the building block of the ISWMP as it focuses on target setting and identification of stakeholders' issues and concern to enable ISWMP to achieve the targets.
- ISWMP: This final step focuses on how to develop an ISWMP utilizing the information collected and generated with the help of the previous three sets of guidelines. This final volume can be used as a stand-alone document to build capacity of experts and policy makers on planning for integrated solid waste management.

Expected Results

Understanding of composite parts of integrated solid waste management to enable preparation of solid waste management plans

Resources	Sustainability
All four volumes are readily available online. Data collection is required.	Crosscutting themes include livelihoods and alternative revenue base.

Pointers for Implementation

The fourth volume can be read as a stand-alone document to guide the preparation of ISWMPs.

References

Each volume can be accessed here: http://www.unep.org/ietc/InformationResources/Publications/tabid/56265/Default.aspx

Examples

Each volume provides a range of examples depending on the thematic area. As the documents have been designed as training manual, each section includes a detailed description of key concepts, methodologies, and practice followed by example boxes or case studies to illustrate each theme.

Waste and Climate Change

Tool: Waste and Climate Change: Global Trends and Strategy Framework	United Nations Environment Programme (UNEP)

Objectives

Promote sustainable waste management in accordance with the waste management hierarchy and reduce greenhouse gas (GHG) emissions from the waste management sector

Approach

The document provides a comprehensive introduction and detailed explanation of the emerging global trends and issues relating to waste and climate change. This includes understanding the relationship between waste and GHG emissions, global trends in waste generation and management, and the climate impacts of waste management practices including

- Landfill,
- Thermal treatment,
- Mechanical biological treatment,
- Composting and anaerobic digestion (of source separated organic waste),
- Recycling, and
- Waste prevention.

The framework includes reference to international initiatives such as the Clean Development Mechanism (CDM) and is followed by guidance to assist in the development of a strategy framework to promote sustainable waste management.

Steps

Strategy Framework.

- Vision
- Goals
- Guiding Principles
- Functions
- Actions

Summary of Approach:

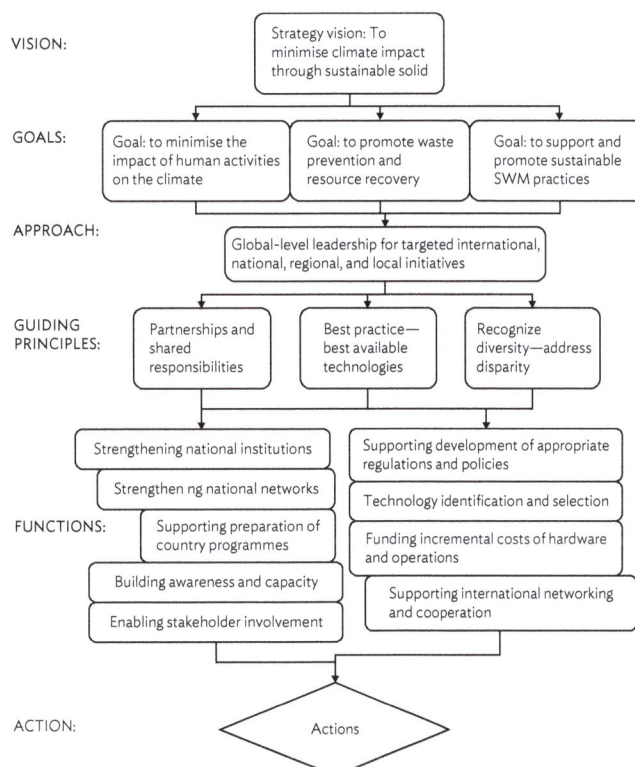

Source: UNEP. Waste and Climate Change: Global Trends and Strategy Framework.

Tool: Waste and Climate Change: Global Trends and Strategy Framework

United Nations Environment Programme (UNEP)

Expected Results

- Improved understanding of current initiatives of solid waste management and how this relates to climate change.
- Improved understanding of the steps involved in calculating GHG emissions derived from waste and development of management plans with reference to existing international initiatives.
- Improved understanding of potential value addition for waste management
- Identification of priority actions aligned with both climate change mitigation and the waste hierarchy.

Resources	Sustainability
Limited technical specialist inputs required during the research and preparation phases. Design and implementation of plans require specialist inputs. Data collection is required.	• Improved accounting of emissions as it relates to waste and preparation of reduction strategies, and can be linked to performance and monitoring and evaluation frameworks. • Cobenefits of waste management and climate change

Pointers for Implementation

This reference document has been prepared as a means of advancing global discussion around waste management and climate change. It provides a useful overview of the technical issues and key concepts of waste and climate change. It should not be seen as a static document but as a relevant reference source.

Executive summary is available in English, Japanese, and Spanish.

Reference

The document can be accessed here: http://www.unep.org/ietc/InformationResources/Publications/WasteandClimateChange/tabid/79353/Default.aspx

Examples

The document provides reference to current practices globally throughout. It also includes technical examples for calculating GHG emissions associated with waste.

Municipal Solid Waste Management

Tool: Social Assessment and Public Participation in Municipal Solid Waste Management	World Bank

Objectives

To provide guidance to central, municipal, and private sector agencies in conducting a social assessment and ensuring appropriate levels of public participation in the planning and implementation of municipal solid waste management (MSWM)

Approach/Summary

The tool kit is intended to provide guidance to social scientists and public participation professionals responsible for carrying out social analysis and/or public participation activities in MSWM. The tool kit is presented in two parts. The first provides an introduction to the tools and clarifies key terms. The second provides detailed explanations and guidance on how to carry out social assessment and its supporting elements: affordability and willingness to pay surveys, community consultation associated with site selection and siting, and engagement strategy and support mechanism for waste pickers and those within the informal sector deriving a livelihood from waste. The tool kit is supported by technical annexes that provide examples of household survey questionnaires and community engagement resources.

A social assessment aims to

- anticipate any social effects of changes by MSWM project;
- involve all social groups and stakeholders affected by changes in the planning of MSWM system improvements;
- manage the changes in a positive process of social development; and
- provide a framework for dialogue on development priorities among social groups, civil society, different levels of government, and other stakeholders.

A social assessment in the context of an investment around MSWM is a form of feasibility study that supports the analysis undertaken in the economic, financial, technical, and environmental sectors. It provides and enables the identification of key stakeholders and relationships between stakeholders, and helps provide better understanding of social norms and behaviors within a community. It supports the preparation of a needs assessment that enables user needs and service preferences to be identified and prioritized.

Sustainability appraisal looks at the potential social risks associated with a project and explores how to address them in order to achieve the project's development objectives. Social risks may range from the obvious, such as involuntary resettlement as well as social and political tensions, to more subtle impacts, such as institutional reforms that affect access to goods and services. Social risks can be broken into five categories: vulnerability, country risks, political economy risks, institutional risks, and exogenous risks. Institutional risks include inappropriate institutional arrangements, weak governance, complexity, and low capacity. Finally, exogenous risks include regional conflicts or macroeconomic changes.

Steps

The parameters taken into account for social assessment are as follows:

- Social Diversity and Gender
- Institutions, Rules, and Behavior
- Stakeholders
- Participation
- Social Risk

Designing effective MSWM strategies or plans requires an understanding of the social diversity and behavioral aspects as well as other characteristics of the key stakeholders. These aspects affect the patterns of materials use, waste generation, and waste disposal of the population, and the associated needs and demands, as well as user and community-based organization and participation in MSWM, community-based waste management activities; and the social conditions of solid waste workers. The considerations are

- waste generation,
- waste disposal,
- solid waste storage and reduction at source,
- siting waste transfer stations and landfills, and
- solid waste recycling.
- Gender and poverty can also play an important role in the entire process. To incorporate stakeholders into solid waste management participation of community, vulnerable groups are also identified.

Tool: Social Assessment and Public Participation in Municipal Solid Waste Management	World Bank

Expected Results

- Understanding of appropriate level of public participation in the planning and implementation of MSWM
- Identification of key stakeholders relevant to MSWM
- Identification of potential risks and impacts to various social groups as related to implementing MSWM initiatives.

Resources

- Resources required for data collection including surveys therefore enumerators and survey teams required.
- Data analysis and technical inputs may require social, gender, and poverty expert; economist; and institutional specialist.

Sustainability

- Linkages between livelihoods and MSWM and quality of life are important considerations to the green city agenda.
- Improved solid waste management must consider livelihoods and potential impacts, in addition to spatial considerations such as access to land, long-term center expansion, and land use patterns.

Pointers for Implementation

- Consider assessment against crosscutting theme of alternative energy supply, climate change mitigation, green infrastructure, and livelihoods.
- The annexes provided include sample terms of reference, household questionnaires, and moderator notes for focus group discussions and semistructured interviews.

Reference

The tool kit can be accessed here: http://siteresources.worldbank.org/INTUSWM/Resources/463617-1202332338898/socialassesstoolkit.pdf

Examples

Case study summary boxes are provided throughout document and include Iran, an international study by the Swiss Federal Institute for Environmental Science and Technology, and Guinea.

Waste Management Scoreboard

Tool: Integrated Waste Management Scoreboard	United Nations Environment Programme (UNEP)

Objectives

The main aim of Integrated Waste Management Scoreboard is to improve municipal solid waste management practices through establishing a means of measuring performance. The scoreboard is a planning tool that provides a framework and approach for evaluating existing municipal solid waste management programs and systems.

It can be used in a variety of ways. As a problem-solving tool, it enables the identification of problem areas in solid waste management and appropriate solutions to be developed. Similarly, it can enable innovative solutions to be recognized and rewarded through an awards program. The latter provides opportunities for enhanced knowledge sharing and transfer and thus replicability of practices.

Approach

The integrated waste management scoreboard provides a methodology for evaluating municipal solid waste programs and systems at the national, provincial, regional, municipal, community, and institutional levels. It uses a points-based system and performance indicators that are based on principles of integrated waste management. The task of reviewing and scoring of performance can be undertaken by an individual or a study team.

The scoreboard recognizes the linkages across tiers of government and application of the principles of sustainable development and the waste management hierarchy. Broadly, this means that the role of national government, and how this is cascaded down to other tiers of government, is framed within the acceptance that national government ought to develop and enact legislation and policies that promote and ensure protection of the environment, to establish an agency or department to implement these programs, and to perform pertinent research and development.

Steps

Flowchart for Integrated Waste Management Scorecard

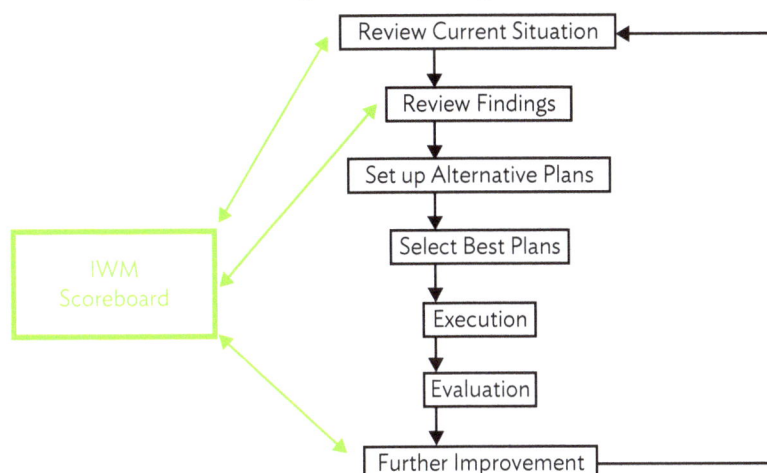

```
                    ┌──────────────────────────┐
                    │  Review Current Situation │◄──────────┐
                    └──────────────────────────┘           │
                                 │                          │
                                 ▼                          │
                    ┌──────────────────────┐                │
                    │   Review Findings     │                │
                    └──────────────────────┘                │
                                 │                          │
                                 ▼                          │
                    ┌──────────────────────┐                │
                    │ Set up Alternative Plans │             │
                    └──────────────────────┘                │
  ┌──────────────┐               │                          │
  │     IWM      │               ▼                          │
  │  Scoreboard  │  ┌──────────────────────┐                │
  └──────────────┘  │   Select Best Plans   │               │
                    └──────────────────────┘                │
                                 │                          │
                                 ▼                          │
                    ┌──────────────────────┐                │
                    │      Execution        │               │
                    └──────────────────────┘                │
                                 │                          │
                                 ▼                          │
                    ┌──────────────────────┐                │
                    │      Evaluation       │               │
                    └──────────────────────┘                │
                                 │                          │
                                 ▼                          │
                    ┌──────────────────────┐                │
                    │  Further Improvement  │───────────────┘
                    └──────────────────────┘
```

Step 1: Initiate the review

Step 2: Prepare for the review

Step 3: Conduct the review/scoring

Step 4: Reporting

Each chapter identifies key considerations and issues by administrative level. Each chapter is consistent in structure, commencing with an overview and followed by institutional framework, waste reduction/avoidance, storage and collection, resource recovery, disposal, and public awareness/education.

Expected Results

- Improved solid waste management system
- Assist in identifying and scoring problematic areas, and informing management strategies
- Consistent assessment framework and scoring approach

Resources

Figure I-2 of the document provides a table identifying the relevant persons to undertake the evaluation.

Sustainability

Regular evaluations assist in improving efficiency of practice and institutions through identification of areas requiring improvement and monitoring of performance.

Pointers for Implementation

The guidelines are set out by administrative or implementing agency level, for example international, national, state/regional, municipal, and community. This is useful as it ensures waste is understood in the context of administrative functions, roles, and responsibilities.

Reference

The Scoreboard can be accessed here: http://www.unep.or.jp/Ietc/Publications/spc/IWM_scoreboard-binder.pdf

Examples

An integrated solid waste management framework is included in addition to completed scorecards at each administrative level. The content of each scorecard reflects the key components of the main document and attributes points to each feature.

Solid Waste E-resources

World Bank

Tool: World Bank Solid Waste Portal	Online reference

Objectives

To provide necessary support and guidance to develop sustainable waste management approaches and projects, including leveraging finance and involving the private sector

Approach

Resources provided are broken into seven thematic areas:

- Solid Waste Management Strategic Planning
- Institutional Capacity Building
- Financial Capacity Building
- Analysis of Technology Choices
- Private Sector Involvement
- Community Initiatives
- Environmental Issues

Each thematic area is explained, and a summary of available resources and tools listed including a further reading section.

Summary of Resources

Solid Waste Management Strategic Planning

- Social Assessment and Public Participation in Municipal Solid Waste Management
- US EPA/RTI Holistic Decision Model for Solid Waste Systems (pdf). S.A. Thorneloe, K.A. Weitz, J. Jambeck. Oct. 2005.
- Strategic Planning Guide for Municipal Solid Waste Management (pdf). Environmental Resources Management (ERM), 2004.
- Practical Guidebook on Strategic Planning in Municipal Solid Waste. World Bank and Cities of Change, 2003.

Related presentations:

- "Waste Collection Planning Tool: Cost Analysis of Collection Options." (pdf) Sandra Cointreau, World Bank, 2005.
- "Private Sector Participation. India: Country Experience and Project Lesson Learnt."(pdf) Shubhagato Dasgupta, World Bank, 2005.

Institutional Capacity Building

- Tool Kit: Private Sector Participation in Municipal Solid Waste Management: Guidance Pack (5 Volumes). S. Cointreau, P. Gopalan, and A. Coad. SKAT, St. Gallen, Switzerland, 2000.
- Video: Solid Waste Outsourcing. C. Hornig. WBI Training Course, January, 2005.
- Presentation: Private Sector Participation in Developing Countries." (pdf) S. Cointreau. March 2005
- Regional Approaches in Waste Disposal: Solid Waste Sanitary Landfill Primer
- How to capture economies of scale

Financial Capacity Building

- COSEPRE: Costs of Urban Cleaning Services

Analysis of Technology Choices

- UNEP Sourcebook of Environmentally Sound Technologies

Private Sector Involvement

- Tool Kit: Private Sector Participation in Municipal Solid Waste Management: Guidance Pack (5 Volumes). S. Cointreau, P. Gopalan, and A. Coad. SKAT, St. Gallen, Switzerland, 2000.

Community Initiatives

Environmental Issues

- Urban solid waste management—This link includes guidance on strategic planning, institutional and financial arrangements, technology assessment, privatization, community-based initiatives, and occupational health and safety of solid waste workers.

Tool: World Bank Solid Waste Portal	Online reference

- Urban environmental management—This link includes environmental tool kits and references on environmental issues of various siting and technology options.
- Urban environmental regulatory and economic instruments framework—This link provides guidance on useful regulation and economic instruments that could motivate improved environmental outcomes during provision of solid waste services.
- Urban environmental consultation with communities—This link provides guidance on public participation in siting, facility design, operational aspects of solid waste service delivery, and addresses special issues related to waste picking and recycling communities.

Practical Guidebook on Strategic Planning in Municipal Waste Management

Expected Results

- Clear understanding of integrated solid waste management
- Prepare solid waste strategic plan
- Identify sustainable solid waste management options and potential financing sources
- Assess solid waste management options and identify green development responses

Reference

The website can be accessed here: http://go.worldbank.org/A5TFX56L50

United Nations Environment Programme

Tool: UNEP Waste Management	Online reference

Objectives

To provide information and support to sustainable waste management through online resource.

Approach

The website has five main thematic areas:

- Demonstration/Pilot projects
- Technology support
- Capacity Building
- Secretariat of Global Partnership for Waste Management (GPWM)
- Eco-towns

Summary of Resources

The thematic areas fulfill two functions: first, showcasing project examples and outlining the purpose of GPWM; and second, sign posting users to available tool kits and guidelines (most are present under technology support and/or capacity building).

Expected Results

- Awareness of available resources, and current and emerging good practice.

Reference

The website can be accessed here: http://www.unep.org/ietc/OurWork/WasteManagement/tabid/56239/Default.aspx

4.6   Transport

Transport Emissions Evaluation Model

Tool: Transport Emissions Evaluation Models for Projects (TEEMP)	Available online Clean Air Initiative

Objectives

To enable estimation of emissions in both project and nonproject scenarios using the sketch models and to evaluate short- to long-term impacts of projects; and to primarily evaluate the impacts of transport projects on carbon dioxide emissions and, to some extent, air pollutant emissions using data gathered during project feasibility and actual operations. The TEEMP tools have been developed in such a way that they require available and easily accessible input data.

Approach

A general emissions estimation manual, as well as project-specific emissions estimation tools are available:

1. Manual for Calculating GHG Benefits of GEF Projects

2. City Sketch Analysis

3. Pedestrian Projects

4. Bike Share projects

5. Bikeways projects

6. Rural Roads Improvement

7. Urban Roads Improvement

8. Rural Expressways

9. LRT/MRT Projects

10. BRTS Projects

11. Railway Projects

12. Commuter Strategies

13. Pricing Strategies

14. Eco-Driving

15. PAYD Insurance

The tools and the manual are also available from the GEF-STAP website.

The TEEMP enables rapid assessment of a transport project's CO_2 impacts and give reasonable direction for action and alternate options evaluation.

Steps

Users are able to select tools most relevant to individual situation. Each tool provides support for low-carbon and emission transport options.

TEEMP tools use flexible spreadsheet "sketch" models to enable estimation of emissions in both "project" and "nonproject" scenarios.

Tool: Transport Emissions Evaluation Models for Projects (TEEMP)
Available online
Clean Air Initiative

Expected Results

- Integrated transport planning
- Climate change mitigation and adaptation planning
- Improved air quality and urban environment

Resources

- A combination of expertise is required—nontechnical to read and develop an overarching understanding of key issues to be applied at the policy level, and specialist technical expertise to assist in the calculation and collection of emissions data, and in the preparation of an inventory and monitoring framework.
- TEEMP predominantly evaluates the impacts of transport projects on CO_2 emissions and, to a lesser extent, air pollutants (particulate matter and nitrogen oxides).

Sustainability

- Integrates emission planning with multiple modes and approaches to transport provision
- Provides the basis to establish emissions baseline and performance indicators to monitor progress

Pointers for Implementation

Available via the Clean Air Initiative portal, this "one-stop shop" provides relevant, easy to use, and accessible resources for emissions and transport planning. In those cities where greenhouse gas inventory or emissions are yet to be undertaken, these tools provide a good starting point highlighting key considerations and data requirements.

The website also includes a guidance manual that provides a step-by-step guide for developing emissions baseline, and for impact estimation and calibration of transport projects.

References

The tool can be accessed here: http://cleanairinitiative.org/portal/TEEMPTool

Additional resources: http://www.stapgef.org/

Examples

Not applicable.

Rapid Assessment of City Emissions

Tool: Rapid Assessment of City Emissions (RACE) from transport and energy	Reference

Objectives

To develop a rapid assessment tool for energy use and emissions (air pollutants and carbon dioxide) for different future scenarios and identify priorities for intervention in cities

Approach

The tool will be applied to four pilot cities: Colombo in Sri Lanka, Ho Chi Minh City in Viet Nam, Ahmedabad in India, and Dalian in the People's Republic of China. A base scenario will be built that includes a baseline year and the next 20 years, makes use of available master plans and existing data for the city, and covering land use and transport integration, and energy use (industrial, commercial, residential, and transport). The data will then be supported by the preparation of geographic information system (GIS) maps demonstrating various scenarios to identify priority interventions.

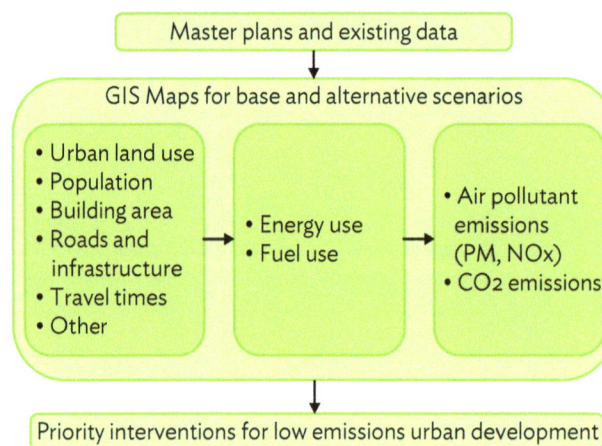

The RACE tool builds on based on Activity–Structure–Intensity–Fuel methodology for calculating transport emissions.

Steps

- Preparation of GIS database that aims at priority interventions for low-emissions urban development.
- Two components—building and transport—are being considered.
- For building assessment parameters such as built-up density, floor area ratio is taken into account, which gives final result in terms of emission per building.
- The transport sector aims at calculating passenger transport emission. This incorporates four parameters—population density, modal share of vehicles, fuel efficiency, and emission factor per mode and fuel per pollutant.

Expected Results

- Increased understanding of interrelationship between transport, land use planning, and emissions.
- Comparative analysis of scenarios based on changes in transport and land use planning and identification of priority intervention areas
- Improved policy to support low emission development
- Understanding the impact of urban development on energy use and emissions, and quickly identifying priorities for intervention
- Increasing the potential to access funds and communicate with investors
- Improving cooperation between relevant government agencies

Resources	Sustainability
RACE tool is still in its pilot stage; however, GIS requirements may limit future and/or wider application.	• Integrates emissions and urban planning • Supports strategic planning (up to 20-year time horizon)

Pointers for Implementation

RACE tool can provide useful framework. Currently in its pilot stage, the tool is not yet available for wider public use.

Reference

The tool can be accessed here: http://cleanairinitiative.org/portal/projects/lowemissioncities

Examples

Application to four pilot cities: Colombo in Sri Lanka, Ho Chi Minh City in Viet Nam, Ahmedabad in India, and Dalian in the People's Republic of China

E-resources

Tool: Clean Air Portal	Online resource

Objectives

Clean Air Asia was established in 2001 as the premier air quality network for Asia by the Asian Development Bank, the World Bank, and the United States Agency for International Development. Its mission is to promote better air quality and livable cities by translating knowledge into policies and actions that reduce air pollution and greenhouse gas emissions from the transport, energy, and other sectors.

Projects and activities are aimed at achieving the following outcomes:

- Strengthened and harmonized regional and national policies and standards
- Enhanced national and local frameworks for sound policies, programs, and urban development
- Increased awareness and access to information, tools, and partners.

Approach

A comprehensive website that provides up-to-date and consolidated information on current projects and activities, upcoming events, and relevant news articles.

Information on the website is provided at both a general level relevant to all geographies as well as to "country networks" that include the People's Republic of China, India, Indonesia, Nepal, Pakistan, the Philippines, Sri Lanka, and Viet Nam.

Membership to the Clean Air Asia is open to all following registration. Membership enables full access to all resources on the website.

Summary of Resources

The website is structured by thematic areas. Of most relevance to users of this tool kit are country networks, communities, and Knowledgebase sections.

The Knowledgebase section enables users to search or filter by city, topic, policy, organization, project and programs, and also provides links and reference to further training and external resources.

The communities section is structured by themes or communities of practice (CoPs) and include

- Air quality and cobenefits
- Sustainable transport
- Network of city networks
- Clean air scorecard
- Center and country networks
- Green freight discussions
- Only the first two CoPs are available to all members; the rest require an invitation to join.
- The country networks section provides information specific to each country as well as a summary of key initiatives.

Expected Results

- Understanding of current clean air and low-carbon development initiatives within Asia
- Access to up-to-date training and support resources relevant to practitioners and government workers

Reference

Clean Air Asia's website is at: www.cleanairasia.org

4.7   Energy

Sustainable Energy Handbook

Tool: Sustainable Energy Handbook: A handbook for cities and towns in developing countries	ICLEI, UN-Habitat, UNEP

Objectives

To assist local government staff and decision makers in the preparation of sustainable energy and climate action plans and implementation programs

Approach

A four-chapter handbook with a comprehensive introductory section that sets out the key challenges of energy consumption, climate change, and development in developing countries. The introduction focuses specifically on the role of urban centers and local governments in defining sustainable development.

The handbook provides a step-by-step guide on how to prepare sustainable energy plans supported by case study examples. It also includes a complete chapter outlining additional support resources for local government developing sustainable energy and climate mitigation responses.

Steps

Developing a Sustainable Energy Plan: A 10-Step Process

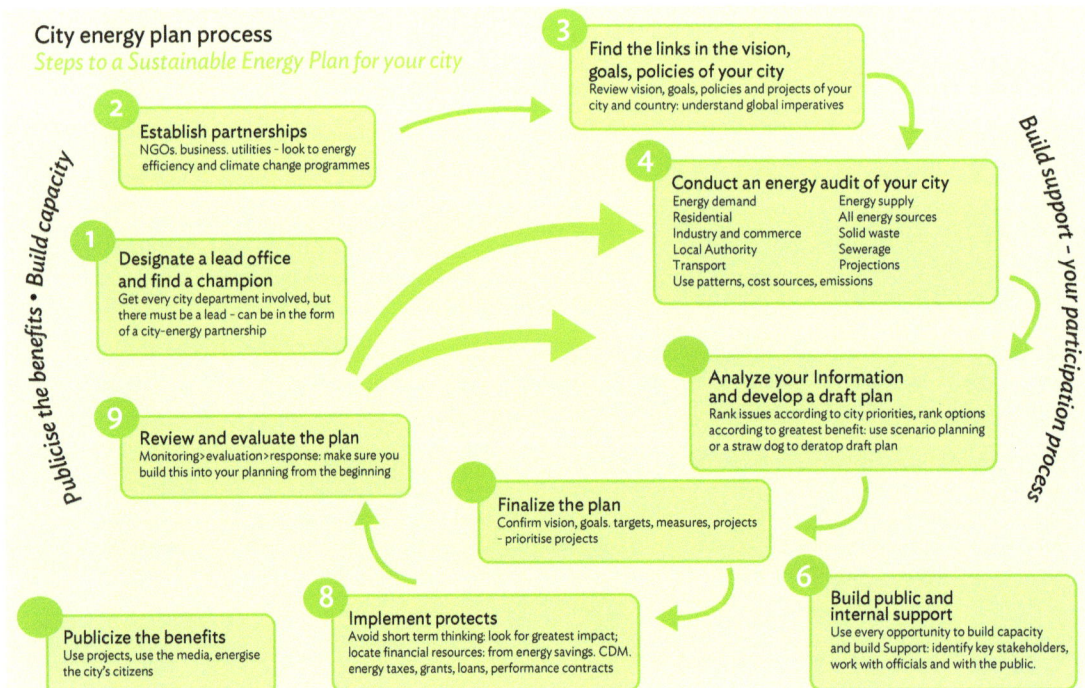

City energy plan process
Steps to a Sustainable Energy Plan for your city

Build capacity • Publicise the benefits

Build support – your participation process

2 Establish partnerships
NGOs. business. utilities - look to energy efficiency and climate change programmes

3 Find the links in the vision, goals, policies of your city
Review vision, goals, policies and projects of your city and country: understand global imperatives

1 Designate a lead office and find a champion
Get every city department involved, but there must be a lead – can be in the form of a city-energy partnership

4 Conduct an energy audit of your city
Energy demand · Energy supply
Residential · All energy sources
Industry and commerce · Solid waste
Local Authority · Sewerage
Transport · Projections
Use patterns, cost sources, emissions

Analyze your Information and develop a draft plan
Rank issues according to city priorities, rank options according to greatest benefit: use scenario planning or a straw dog to deratop draft plan

9 Review and evaluate the plan
Monitoring>evaluation>response: make sure you build this into your planning from the beginning

Finalize the plan
Confirm vision, goals. targets, measures, projects - prioritise projects

Publicize the benefits
Use projects, use the media, energise the city's citizens

8 Implement protects
Avoid short term thinking: look for greatest impact; locate financial resources: from energy savings. CDM. energy taxes, grants, loans, performance contracts

6 Build public and internal support
Use every opportunity to build capacity and build Support: identify key stakeholders, work with officials and with the public.

Tool: Sustainable Energy Handbook:
A handbook for cities and towns in developing countries — ICLEI, UN-Habitat, UNEP

Expected Results

- Comprehensive understanding of sustainable urban energy
- Sustainable urban energy plan
- Local action plan

Resources

The greatest resource is the time of individuals to read, research, collect data, and prepare relevant plans. Implementation of developed plans will require additional resources including technical specialists. The planning process will enable these technical requirements to be identified.

Sustainability

Improving energy efficiency of urban areas, reducing emissions, and undertaking regular monitoring and evaluation of plans and programs contribute to the long-term sustainability of cities and urban areas.

Pointers for Implementation

Each chapter provides a series of questions that act as a prompt to assist considering all issues.

The handbook is effective at sign posting readers where to find additional information as well as support tools.

Reference

The handbook can be accessed here: http://www.unep.org/urban_environment/PDFs/Sustainable_Energy_Handbook.pdf?bcsi_scan_97e98328e2b67804=0&bcsi_scan_filename=Sustainable_Energy_Handbook.pdf

Examples

Each chapter (structured in line with each step) provides detailed case studies demonstrating principles in practice.

Energy Forecasting Framework and Emissions Consensus Tool

Tool: Energy Forecasting Framework and Emissions Consensus Tool (EFFECT)	Energy Sector Management Assistance Program (ESMAP)

Objectives

To forecast greenhouse gas (GHG) emissions from a range of development scenarios, focusing on sectors that contribute to, and are expected to experience, a rapid growth in emissions.

The Energy Forecasting Framework and Emissions Consensus Tool (EFFECT) is an open and transparent modeling tool used to forecast greenhouse gas (GHG) emissions from a range of development scenarios. It focuses on sectors that contribute to, and are expected to experience, a rapid growth in emissions.

Approach

The model was initially developed by the World Bank while working with the Government of India on an analysis of their national energy plan.

EFFECT forecasts GHG emissions for given development scenarios or policy choices. In addition to this, EFFECT enables consensus building among disparate government departments, and forecasts energy balances and amounts of energy generating/consuming assets in a country or sector. EFFECT also produces results for individual sectors such as road transport, agriculture, power, industry, household, and nonresidential sectors.

Steps

Energy Forecasting Framework and Emissions Consensus Tool (EFFECT) has three main steps:

- Development Scenario input data
- Forecast into future
- Scenario GHG emissions

Sectors that are covered by the tool include

- Transport (road and rail)
- Agriculture
- Power
- Industry
- Households
- Nonresidential

Expected Results

- EFFECT thus yields GHG emission forecasts from data about energy-producing and -consuming assets in differing development scenarios and generates immediate results to inform low-carbon planning.
- Sector-specific results to support sector-based low-carbon planning.

Resource	Sustainability
Windows operating system is required.	Publicly available tool that supports scenario planning to support low-carbon planning across multiple sectors. Integration and multisector approaches are key to long-term sustainability.

Pointers for Implementation

A self-paced e-learning course is available through the World Bank Institute (WBI). The course has several modules ranging from the basics of low-carbon development to specific details on how to use EFFECT. Follow the instructions to self-register and access the course using "EFFECT," as the enrollment key. The course is available free of charge.

Reference

The resource can be accessed here: http://esmap.org/EFFECT

Examples

EFFECT has been completed in seven countries: Brazil, the People's Republic of China, India, Indonesia, the Philippines, Poland, and Thailand. Other countries where the tool is being applied include Georgia, Macedonia, Nigeria, and Viet Nam.

Marginal Abatement

Tool: Marginal Abatement Cost Tool (MACTool)	Energy Sector Management Assistance Program (ESMAP)

Objectives

The Marginal Abatement Cost Tool (MACTool) is a transparent, flexible software tool that provides an easy way for building marginal abatement cost curves, and for calculating break-even carbon prices. The user-friendly interface guides users through a simple data entry process that generates marginal abatement cost curves.

Approach

There is a growing demand for low-carbon planning support as governments work toward reducing greenhouse gas emissions and improve energy security. However, low-carbon planning is a complex, iterative process. MACTool helps governments answer the following questions:

- Among available mitigation options, which will be the most efficient and cost-effective?
- What are the potential results associated with each option?
- What does it cost to implement each option?

MACTool helps policymakers compare the costs and benefits of emission reduction options that can be used to build low-carbon scenarios at a national or subnational level. It provides a cost–benefit comparison of these options and an estimate of the incentives needed to make these options attractive for the private sector by calculating **break-even carbon prices**. It also enables governments to assess the total investment needed to shift toward low-carbon growth. MACTool can also be used to test the possibility of a domestic cap and trade system, by exploring which sectors would be likely to respond to a given carbon price.

MACTool builds a reference scenario and low-carbon scenarios for individual low-carbon option. It allows users to schedule investments for low-carbon alternatives along the planning period. It calculates the differential in emissions, investments, costs, and revenues between the scenarios, and generates customized curves that make it easy to visualize options.

Steps

MACTool follows four main steps:

- Input data
- Calculate marginal abatement costs
- Rank marginal abatement costs
- MAC curve and create graphics

Note: Marginal Abatement Cost (MAC): Net Present Value of Costs and Benefits (unique Internal Rate of Return for each option) associated with a mitigation option, divided by the number of tons of CO_2 abated during the period considered.

Expected Results

- Determine volume of investment needed to achieve different sets of mitigation targets
- Preliminary assessment of possible local cap and trade programs

Resources	Sustainability
- Basic computer/laptop - Data collection	- Risk assessment linked to strategic planning and quantification of potential costs as result of actions or nonaction - Supports green economic/low-carbon growth

Pointers for Implementation

MACTool comes with embedded videos providing users with step-by-step guidance on using MACTool. Training is also available via ESMAP.

To access and download the tool, it is necessary to e-mail esmap@worldbank.org

References

The tool can be accessed here: http://esmap.org/MACTool

A further summary of the tool can be accessed here: http://www.esmap.org/sites/esmap.org/files/ESMAP_KES2012_MACTool.pdf

Examples

Countries that have commenced using the MACTool include Brazil, Macedonia, and Viet Nam.

Tool for Rapid Assessment of City Energy

Tool: Tool for Rapid Assessment of City Energy (TRACE)	Energy Sector Management Assistance Program (ESMAP)

Objectives

The Tool for Rapid Assessment of City Energy (TRACE) is a decision-support tool designed to help cities quickly identify underperforming sectors, evaluate improvement and cost-saving potential, and prioritize sectors and actions for energy efficiency (EE) intervention. It covers six municipal sectors: passenger transport, municipal buildings, water and wastewater, public lighting, solid waste, and power and heat.

Approach

TRACE consists of three modules: an energy benchmarking module, which compares key performance indicators (KPIs) among peer cities; a sector prioritization module, which identifies sectors that offer the greatest potential with respect to energy-cost savings; and an intervention selection module, which functions like a "playbook" of tried-and-tested EE measures and helps select locally appropriate EE interventions.

TRACE is designed with the intention to involve city decision makers in the deployment process. It starts with benchmark data collection, goes through an on-location assessment involving experts and decision makers, and ends with a final report to city authorities with recommendations of EE interventions tailored to the city's individual context.

Steps

Energy Benchmarking

TRACE's benchmarking module has a database of 28 KPIs collected from 64 cities. The data are entered into the tool using a simple web-like interface and analyzed in order to benchmark city energy use against a range of peer cities. The peer cities may be selected based on city population, climate, and human development index.

Sector Prioritization

TRACE's sector prioritization module uses "relative energy intensity," "sector energy spending," and "city authority control" to prioritize sectors with the most significant energy efficiency potential. The "sector spending function" allows the user to enter the total amount of money that the city spends in the sector, and the "city authority control" function allows the user to indicate the amount of control that the city authority has in the sector. The "relative intensity function" shows the potential energy efficiency improvement the city may realize if it were to match the average of better-performing cities. Based on these functions, TRACE provides the prioritized list of sectors that the city can engage in order to realize potential energy savings.

Intervention Selection

TRACE contains a set of 59 EE interventions that combine a blend of both high- and strategic-level programs and specific activities that a city can pursue. These recommendations are supported by a database of 191 case studies that link to appropriate resources and tools. Each recommendation is "rated" on three attributes: energy savings potential, first cost, and speed of implementation.

The initial appraisal step enables the user to match city capability to the capabilities required to implement each recommendation. City officials can then select from the set of ranked recommendations.

The energy savings assessment step allows the user to quantify the potential energy savings using spreadsheets that come with TRACE, and the final review process allows the city authorities to assess the viability of recommendations in order to come up with a final list of actions for prioritized sectors.

Expected Results

- Matrix of recommendations based on savings potential, first cost, and speed of implementation.
- Identified list of actions ranked by priority and sector.

Tool: Tool for Rapid Assessment of City Energy (TRACE)	Energy Sector Management Assistance Program (ESMAP)
Resources	**Sustainability**
The tool is available upon request and includes data and information that have been collected and pre-inputted into the tool from the ESMAP database.	• Supports strategic planning at short-, mid-, and long-term time horizons • Enables performance-based assessment to be incorporated into monitoring and evaluation frameworks. • Considers performance at both the sector and city levels to prevent potential harmful incentives.

Pointers for Implementation

A TRACE e-learning course was created in partnership with the World Bank Institute (WBI). WBI requires that users create an account to access the course. When prompted, enter the registration key "trace12."

ESMAP also provides group training to cities or implementing agencies planning to use TRACE. These can be provided in person or via video, depending on resource availability.

ESMAP offers facilitated courses, free of charge, for users planning to use TRACE. These courses are offered online at various times throughout the year.

Reference

The tool can be accessed here: http://esmap.org/TRACE

Examples

Numerous country examples of TRACE tool: Bosnia and Herzegovina, Brazil, Ethiopia, Georgia, Ghana, Indonesia, Kenya, Kosovo, Macedonia, the Philippines, Serbia, Turkey, and Viet Nam.

Energy Efficiency Guide for Industry in Asia

Tool: Energy Efficiency Guide for Industry in Asia

Objectives

The tool kit and guidelines were prepared as a part of Greenhouse Gas Emission Reduction from Industry in Asia and the Pacific (GERIAP) project.

This guide has been developed for Asian companies who want to improve energy efficiency through Cleaner Production and for stakeholders who want to help them.

Approach

The guideline has three main approaches:

- Capacity building: National focal points and participating companies receive training on how to apply Cleaner Production to identify energy efficiency options for main energy uses in industry.
- Demonstration of Cleaner Production and energy efficiency: Cleaner Production assessments to find ways to improve energy efficiency were carried out at the participating companies. Options that were technically feasible, financially attractive, and reduced energy and greenhouse gas emissions were implemented, resulting in sector-specific case studies.
- Survey of barriers to energy efficiency: Why do some companies improve energy efficiency while others do not? A survey assessed the financial, technical, cultural, and other factors affecting businesses, resulting in proposed solutions to overcome the most important regional and national barriers in Asia.

Steps

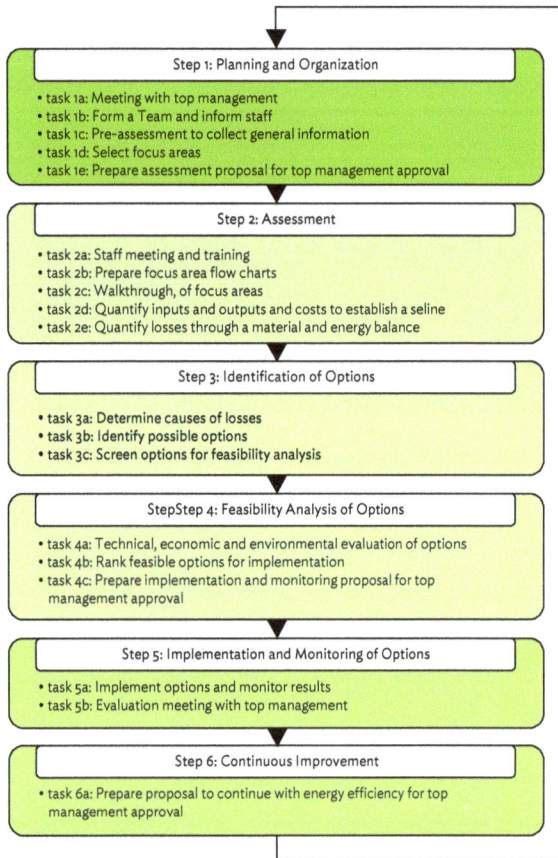

A six-step framework, as highlighted, sets out the tasks and steps companies must follow to improve energy efficiency.

The main steps are as follows:

- Planning and Organization
- Assessment
- Identification of Options
- Feasibility Analysis of Options
- Implementation and Monitoring of Options
- Continuous Improvement

Step 1: Planning and Organization
- task 1a: Meeting with top management
- task 1b: Form a Team and inform staff
- task 1c: Pre-assessment to collect general information
- task 1d: Select focus areas
- task 1e: Prepare assessment proposal for top management approval

Step 2: Assessment
- task 2a: Staff meeting and training
- task 2b: Prepare focus area flow charts
- task 2c: Walkthrough, of focus areas
- task 2d: Quantify inputs and outputs and costs to establish a seline
- task 2e: Quantify losses through a material and energy balance

Step 3: Identification of Options
- task 3a: Determine causes of losses
- task 3b: Identify possible options
- task 3c: Screen options for feasibility analysis

StepStep 4: Feasibility Analysis of Options
- task 4a: Technical, economic and environmental evaluation of options
- task 4b: Rank feasible options for implementation
- task 4c: Prepare implementation and monitoring proposal for top management approval

Step 5: Implementation and Monitoring of Options
- task 5a: Implement options and monitor results
- task 5b: Evaluation meeting with top management

Step 6: Continuous Improvement
- task 6a: Prepare proposal to continue with energy efficiency for top management approval

Expected Results

- Improved energy efficiency through clean production methods
- Improved understanding of stakeholder engagement to support energy efficiency initiatives

Resources	Sustainability
No specific resources required. Time-based only.	Clean production methods and improved energy efficiency contribute to the long-term sustainability of both the industry sector involved and wider environment.

Pointers for Implementation

- While aimed at the industrial private sector, the principles applied to encourage cultural change and improve energy efficiency can be applied to broader government or institutional context.
- The web reference below provides full access to the available resources. This includes a user guide that can be downloaded and used as reference document. This user guide also sets out where additional information can be sourced.

Reference

The guide is available here: www.energyefficiencyasia.org

Examples

Nine Asian countries participated: Bangladesh, the People's Republic of China, India, Indonesia, Mongolia, the Philippines, Sri Lanka, Thailand, and Viet Nam.

E-resources

Renewable Energy and Energy Efficiency Partnership

Tool: Renewable Energy and Energy Efficiency Partnership (REEEP)	Online resource

Objectives

The Renewable Energy and Energy Efficiency Partnership (REEEP) digital library offers an array of information in the field of Renewable Energy and Energy Efficiency. These range from policy papers and case studies to presentations that are produced by REEEP-funded projects spanning the entire globe. New information is added regularly.

Approach

An online search engine that can filter results by technology, geography, and project sector/theme. Categories are as follows.

Energy Efficiency

- Energy efficiency (general)
- Agriculture
- Appliances
- Buildings
- Distribution and metering
- Electrical
- Energy generation and transmission
- Industry
- Secondary fuel switch (e.g., electricity with steam)
- Thermal
- Transportation
- Utility-Demand side

Renewable Energy

- Renewable energy (general)
- Biofuels
- Biogas
- Biomass
- Fuel cell
- Geothermal
- Hydropower
- Hydrogen energy
- Marine energy
- Solar photovoltaic
- Solar thermal electricity
- Solar thermal heat
- Wind energy

General EE and RE

Project Sector

- Energy Efficiency (EE)
- Renewable Energy (RE)
- EE and RE

Project Theme

- Finance and Business
- Policy and Regulation
-

Project Duration

Region Filter

- Central and Eastern Europe*
- East Asia
- Latin America and the Caribbean
- North America*
- The Russian Federation and Former Soviet Union*
- Southern Africa
- South Asia
- Southeast Asia and the Pacific

*REEEP no longer supports projects in these regions, and information may be outdated.

Summary of Resources

Over 200 reference documents, guides, and case studies are available.

Expected Results

- Advance Energy community of practice
- Platform for knowledge transfer and good practice
- Effective and efficient online system

References

The tool kits can be accessed here: http://www.reeep.org/toolkits-and-outcomes and http://www.reegle.info/projectoutputs

ESMAP

Tool: Energy Sector Management Assistance Program (ESMAP)	Online resource

Objectives

The Energy Sector Management Assistance Program (ESMAP) is a global knowledge and technical assistance program administered by the World Bank. Its mission is to assist low- and middle-income countries in increasing know-how and institutional capacity to achieve environmentally sustainable energy solutions for poverty reduction and economic growth.

Approach

Focus areas:

- Energy Security
  To help ensure long-term energy security, countries are looking closely at renewable energy, efficiency practices and technologies, diversification of supply, and improved sector performance. ESMAP assists its clients in carrying out energy assessments and developing strategies to enhance sector planning, regulation, and governance.
- Energy Access
  About 1.4 billion of the world's people still lack access to electricity, and poor households spend $20 billion a year on low-quality, fuel-based lighting. Respiratory diseases are widespread among the 2.7 billion people who still rely on biomass for cooking, with women and children the hardest hit. ESMAP supports initiatives to reduce energy poverty by expanding access to modern, safe, affordable, and sustainable energy services. ESMAP's energy access work covers electrification and household energy needs in rural areas and for the urban poor.
- Climate Change
  Climate change will directly affect energy resource endowments, infrastructure, and transportation, as well as energy demand. ESMAP assists client countries in integrating climate change mitigation and adaptation options into energy sector planning. ESMAP also supports the scale-up of renewable energy through resource assessments, strategy development, and policy and institutional development.

Summary of Resources

Five main areas:

- Publications
  This section includes all publications supported by ESMAP, including technical reports, briefing notes, workshop proceedings, brochures, and case studies aimed at promoting environmentally sustainable energy solutions for poverty reduction and economic growth.
- Knowledge Tools
  ESMAP has contributed significantly to the development of knowledge tools to guide decision making about climate change mitigation and low-carbon growth. Such modeling and planning tools help generate consensus on data and assumptions among a wide range of stakeholders, and the outputs provide a valuable evidence base upon which to define priorities and design policy responses. Demand from countries for these services is significant and growing, and ESMAP already has experience helping to implement these tools in 18 countries.
- Tool Kits
  – Hands-on Energy Adaptation Toolkit (HEAT)
  – Large-Scale Residential Energy Efficiency Programs Based on Compact Fluorescent Lamps (CFLs)
  – Community Development Tool Kit
- Promotional Materials
- E-bulletins

Expected Results

- Improved understanding and awareness of energy efficiency, environmental sustainability, and related topics.
- Improved capacity to prepare and undertake assessments, and develop strategy and policy.

Reference

The website can be accessed here: https://www.esmap.org/

4.8   Built Environment

Leadership in Energy and Environmental Design

Tool: Leadership in Energy and Environmental Design (LEED)	U.S. Green Building Council

Objectives

The Leadership in Energy and Environmental Design (LEED) is a voluntary, consensus-based, market-driven program that provides third-party verification of green buildings.

LEED-certified buildings are designed to

- lower operating costs and increase asset value;
- reduce waste sent to landfills;
- conserve energy and water;
- be healthier and safer for occupants;
- reduce harmful greenhouse gas emissions; and
- qualify for tax rebates, zoning allowances, and other incentives in hundreds of cities.

Approach

LEED is an online resource that enables registered users to manage and track progress of submitted projects for certification. LEED online is designed to

- submit documentation for review,
- document compliance with LEED credit requirements,
- submit technical queries regarding LEED credits, and
- track progress toward LEED certification.

The LEED credit-based rating system is based on the following building and design elements:

- Sustainable Sites: There are certain prerequisites to reduce negative impacts on water, soil, and air quality. Site Selection (location), Urban Redevelopment (development in urban areas with existing infrastructure), Brownfield Redevelopment (rehabilitate damaged sites), Alternative transportation (reduce impacts due to automobile use), Reduced Site Disturbance (conserve and restore damaged areas), Stormwater Management (curtail stormwater runoff on-site), Landscape and Exterior Design to reduce heat islands and Light Pollution reduction (eliminate light trespass from the building site).
- Water Efficiency: This credit can be gained through Water-efficient Landscaping, innovative wastewater technologies, and maximizing water use efficiency.
- Energy and Atmosphere: To attain this intent, the following steps can be taken—verify and ensure that fundamental building elements and systems are designed, installed, and calibrated to operate as intended; establish minimum level of energy efficiency; reduce use of ozone-depleting products; and optimize energy performance, accountability and optimization of energy and water consumption, and use of green power.
- Materials and Resources: The prerequisites for this credit include facilitating the reduction of waste generated by buildings, building reuse, storage and collection of recyclables, construction waste management, resource reuse, and use of local and rapidly renewable materials.
- Indoor Environmental Quality (IEQ): Better IEQ performance helps sustain long-term occupant health and comfort. This can be achieved through carbon dioxide monitoring, increased ventilation effectiveness, construction indoor air quality management plan, reduced indoor air contaminants, nonexposure to hazardous chemicals, thermal comfort, and introduction of daylight and view.
- Innovation Credits and Design or Build Process: The design team is awarded points for exceptional performance above requirements set by LEED Green Buildings.

Tool: Leadership in Energy and Environmental Design (LEED)   U.S. Green Building Council

Steps

The building accreditation process involves five steps, all of which can be undertaken online. These steps are summarized below:

LEED certification involves five primary steps

1. Choose which rating system to use. Keep in mind, some projects clearly fit the defined scope of ore LEED rating system; others may be eligible for two or more.

2. Register. The LEED process begins with registration. Once registration forms are submitted and payment is complete, your project will be accessible in LEED Online.

3. Submit your certification application and pay a certification review fee. Fees differ with project type and size.

4. Review. Await the application review. Review processes differ slightly for each project type.

5. Certify. Receive the certification decision, which you can either accept or appeal. An affirmative decision signifies that your building is now LEED certified.

REGISTER A PROJECT

Search projects

How many points does it take?
The number of points a project earns determines the level of LEED Certification the project will recieve. Learn More ›

CERT 200: LEED Certification: Think Like A Reviewer
Learn how to certify smarter and achieve LEED certification upon preliminary review.
Access the course ›

Expected Results

- Improved energy efficiency of buildings
- Improved neighborhood-scale design
- Internationally benchmarked and recognized accreditation

Resources

- Professional expertise is required to prepare construction/ architectural drawings for submission and assessment and, ultimately, certification.
- Financial costs are incurred to technical drawing preparation and certification.

Sustainability

Better designed buildings and improved energy efficiency improved urban environments. Supported and facilitated by the U.S. Green Building Council.

Pointers for Implementation

- Fees for registration and accreditation are applicable. Price structures will vary, depending on the nature of development.
- The rating system is recognized as an international benchmark for energy-efficient buildings. Design principles of LEED can be applied to a broader context, and inform policy and good practice.
- LEED offers accreditation for Neighborhood Development, which considers a wider context and issues such as land use patterns, connectivity, walkability, and access to alternative modes of transport.

References

Access the full suite of LEED information and rating systems here: http://new.usgbc.org/leed

Examples

LEED is facilitated by the U.S. Green Building Council. The website provides a range of support and information resources for users.

Building Research Establishment Environmental Assessment Method

Tool: Building Research Establishment Environmental Assessment Method (BREEAM)

Objectives

A Building Research Establishment Environmental Assessment Method (BREEAM) assessment uses recognized measures of performance, which are set against established benchmarks, to evaluate a building's specification, design, construction, and use. The measures used represent a broad range of categories and criteria, from energy to ecology. They include aspects related to energy and water use, the internal environment (health and well-being), pollution, transport, materials, waste, ecology, and management processes.

It is delivered by a licensed organization that uses trained assessors to provide

- market recognition for low environmental impact buildings,
- confidence that tried and tested environmental practice is incorporated in the building,
- inspiration to find innovative solutions that minimize the environmental impact,
- a benchmark that is higher than regulation,
- a system to help reduce running costs and improve working and living environments, and
- a standard that demonstrates progress toward corporate and organizational environmental objectives.

Approach

BREEAM establishes an environmental assessment framework and an accreditation system that sets standards for

- Sustainable building design
- Construction and operation
- Prepare measures of performance
- It is a code for a sustainable built environment.

Steps

BREEAM rewards performance above regulation which delivers environmental, comfort, or health benefits as follows:
- Energy: operational energy and carbon dioxide (CO_2)
- Management: management policy, commissioning, site management, and procurement
- Health and Well-being: indoor and external issues (noise, light, air quality, etc.)
- Transport: transport-related CO_2 and location-related factors
- Water consumption and efficiency
- Materials: embodied impacts of building materials, including lifecycle impacts like embodied CO_2
- Waste: construction resource efficiency and operational waste management and minimization
- Pollution: external air and water pollution
- Land Use: type of site and building footprint
- Ecology: ecological value, conservation, and enhancement of the site

Expected Results

- Integration of design principles and standards into urban planning and development documents
- Improved spatial layout and consideration to "lifecycle" of development.

Resources	Sustainability
- Licensed assessors are required for BREEAM accreditation. - Professional expertise is required to prepare construction/architectural drawings for submission and assessment and, ultimately, certification. - Financial costs are incurred in connection with technical drawing preparation and certification.	Better designed buildings and improved energy efficiency improved urban environments. Integration with land use planning and development control

Pointers for Implementation

- Free online training, which is available via the BREEAM website, looks at sustainability principles and planning, and includes guidance on drafting policy.
- BREEAM has developed a code for a sustainable built environment (Europe and Outside Europe). The International (non-Europe) guide provides a conceptual framework for a county that may establish its own green building council and adopt a uniformed approach to sustainable development. This can be accessed via the website.

Reference

The website can be accessed here: http://www.breeam.org/

Examples

European case study examples showcasing residential, commercial, and public use/building examples are provided on the website.

Green Star

Tool: Green Star	Green Building Council of Australia

Objectives

Green Star is an internationally recognized voluntary environmental rating system that evaluates the environmental design and construction of buildings and communities. It was developed for the Australian property industry in order to

- establish a common language;
- set a standard of measurement for built environment sustainability;
- promote integrated, holistic design;
- recognize environmental leadership;
- identify and improve lifecycle impacts; and
- raise awareness of the benefits of sustainable design, construction, and urban planning.

Approach

Green Star Certification is a formal process that involves a project using a Green Star rating tool to guide the design or construction process during which a documentation-based submission is collated as proof of this achievement. Overseen by the Green Building Council of Australia, the certification process includes a validation process by a panel of third-party Certified Assessors. Certification and submission requirements are supported by a technical manual that accompanies each rating tool.

There are numerous rating tools available that cover a range of land uses including residential, commercial, health, and education.

In 2013, a pilot tool for "communities" was released. This tool provides best practice benchmarks and third part verification of the sustainability of community and precinct-wide developments.

Steps

Certification is undertaken in two steps:

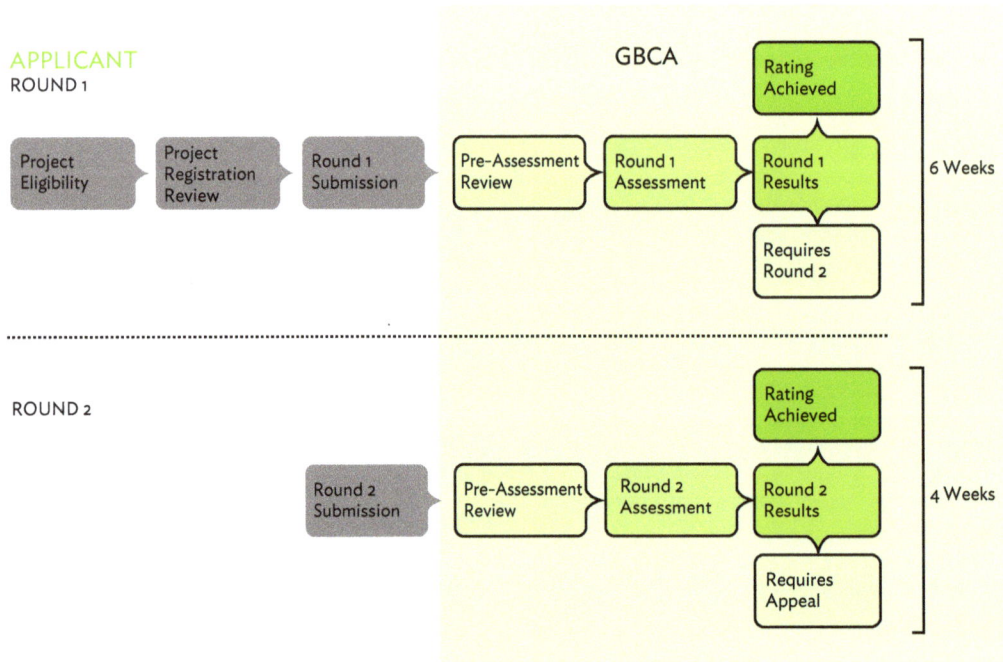

Expected Results

- Improved building design to encourage energy efficiency
- Consideration to building design within urban planning process
- Bench marked building
- Consideration to building/development life cycle

Tool: Green Star	Green Building Council of Australia
Resources	**Sustainability**
Resources and information that explain the certification process; tools are readily available free of charge via the Green Building Council of Australia website. Additional and specialist expertise to prepare the necessary document to enable certification is required. Fees for certification are applicable.	Integrated design that considers all aspects of environmental sustainability; reduced energy consumption, alternative energy, water capture, treatment, and reuse contribute to buildings and development sites becoming more adaptive and sustainable.

Pointers for Implementation

The Green Star rating tool is only applicable to buildings within Australia. However, the technical guidance and principles of good practice and design and use of benchmarks are transferable to other geographies. It can be used as a resource to inform policy and as a model that may be replicated.

References

The tool and all supporting information can be accessed here: http://www.gbca.org.au/green-star/green-star-overview

Examples

The website includes a section on Australian case studies.

4.9   Urban Resilience

Section 2.2 of the tool kit provides a brief introduction to the concept of "urban resilience," outlining how it encompasses climate change adaptation and mitigation and disaster risk reduction elements. This section of the tool inventory thus sets out those tools that can be used under each thematic area. The resource matrix (see Table 4.1) provides a summary of current and available reading and online materials.

Urban Climate Change Resilience (UCCR)

Urban Climate Change Resilience: A Synopsis	Resource document Asian Development Bank

Objectives

The synopsis provides a concise and accessible introduction to urban climate change resilience (UCCR). It outlines key principles and concepts providing insights and lessons learned from implementation.

Its audience include ADB project officers, consultants, and partners who are interested in UCCR.

Approach

The synopsis is structured in six sections.

Sections 1 and 2 provide an introduction to and describe the principles of UCCR.

Section 3 describes the resilience planning processes that underpin UCCR action.

Section 4 profiles specific examples of investments and projects that demonstrate the qualities of UCCR.

Sections 5 and 6 highlight the importance of knowledge for UCCR and further reading.

Expected Results

• Understanding of UCCR approach, application, and principles.

References

Available from ADB website.

4.10   Climate Change Adaptation

Adaptation Wizard

Tool: The Adaptation Wizard	United Kingdom Climate Impacts Programme (UKCIP)

Objectives

The Adaptation Wizard is an action-oriented tool with the core aim of converting theory into practical action. It is a generic decision-support tool that encompasses all elements of climate risk assessment and adaptation within a single process. The Wizard's design leaves scope for application by a large extent of users. Similarly, its application can be used for a plan, a project, a program, or a policy.

The objective of the Adaptation Wizard is to establish vulnerability to climate change, identify main climate risks, and, based on these, suggest a climate change adaptation strategy.

Approach

The Wizard is structured around a five-step process that users can employ to assess their climate risks and establish an adaptation strategy.

The Adaptation Wizard is founded on several guiding principles of which working in partnership is listed first. However, Adaptation Wizard also adopts the use of SMART (specific, measurable, achievable, results-oriented, and time-bound) objectives and highlights the importance of communicating and framing objectives and outcomes in this manner. SMART is an instructive approach to adopt when undertaking a planning process.

It is also available at no cost to users.

Steps

The five-step process:

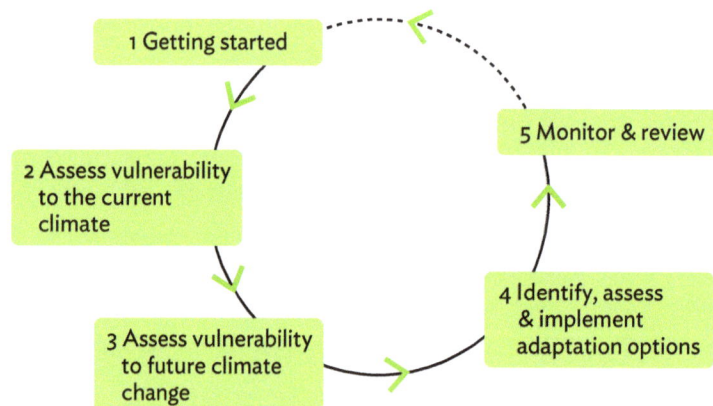

Source: http://www.ukcip.org.uk/wizard/

Tool: The Adaptation Wizard	United Kingdom Climate Impacts Programme (UKCIP)

Expected Results

- Provides a framework and resources to assist in generating the necessary information to prepare adaptation strategy
- Increased knowledge and awareness on what information is required to prepare and maintain adaptation strategy

Resources	Sustainability
Completing the Wizard involves working with colleagues and partners to gather information and answer the questions asked of you. Unless the assessment reveals a need to commission further research to quantify your climate risks or evaluate various adaptation options, completing the Wizard involves few capital costs; the primary cost is time to work through the Wizard, gather information, and answer the questions posed.	The adaptation process is iterative, and keeping a full record of answers informing adaptation planning is critical as is review and updating. The tool provides the framework to support this process that is applicable across administrative, institutional, and community levels.

Pointers for Implementation

The website is highly interactive and includes a series of supporting reference materials. An offline guide to the entire tool can be downloaded.

Commence process with reading the "Principles of Good Adaptation" section.

Reference

The tool can be accessed here: http://www.ukcip.org.uk/wizard/

Examples

Pilot studies specific to Adaptation Wizard are United Kingdom-oriented and include Port of Felixstowe and Midcounties Cooperative.

AdOpt

Tool: AdOpt	United Kingdom Climate Impacts Programme (UKCIP)

Objectives

This tool aims to provide assistance in the identification and selection of adaptation options. It is based on the UKCIP Risk, Uncertainty and Decision-Making Framework, which sets the range of the available adaptation options. The tool provides a simple checklist establishing core principles for good adaptation decisions.

Approach

Provides an overview of why adaptation is relevant, clearly setting out the guiding principles to adaptation planning including identification of stakeholders and dealing with uncertainty.

An overview of four adaptation options:

- No-regrets adaptation options
- Low-regrets adaptation options
- Win–win adaptation options
- Flexible or adaptive management options

Captured in the following figure:

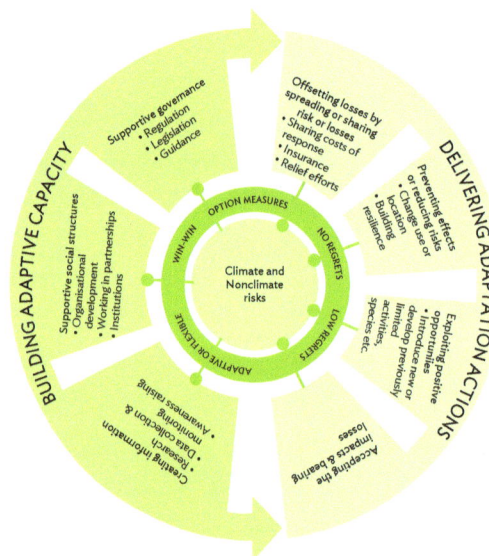

- Adaptation is iterative, and therefore reassessment of options is required. This process is supported by identifying lessons learned, innovations in technology, and increased understanding of risks and science.

Steps

This tool supports the use of other UKCIP tools and should be read as a guidance note.

Expected Results

- Support to decision and policy makers to identify and appraise effectiveness of adaptation measures
- Improved understanding of the nature and characteristics of adaptation in the context of climate risk

Resources	Sustainability
Available online. Time of staff or persons developing adaptation strategy to read, understand, and complete assessment process.	A support tool that enables users to identify adaptation responses and develop a monitoring and evaluation framework to ensure projects are not static and thus are adaptive, more resilient, and sustainable.

Pointers for Implementation

This tool should be considered a companion to the other UKCIP tools such as Adaptation Wizard and the Risk, Uncertainty and Decision-Making Framework.

Reference

The tool can be accessed here: http://www.ukcip.org.uk/adopt/

Examples

Appendixes 1 and 2 provide example adaptation checklists which identify key principles that are in keeping with good adaptation decisions.

Local Climate Impact Profile (LCLIP)

Tool: Local Climate Impacts Profile (LCLIP)	United Kingdom Climate Impacts Programme (UKCIP)

Objectives

The Local Climate Impacts Profile (LCLIP) tool is used to assess a locality's vulnerability to severe weather events. The evaluation is meant to state how the effects of climate change will affect local authority assets, infrastructure, and capacity to deliver services.

Approach

UKCIP has developed a user guide[16] for councils to refer to when completing their LCLIP. The user guide sets out the rationale for preparing an LCLIP and highlights the main stages in the process then providing a "how to" section and explanation of what the expected outputs will be.

Using a four-step process (project planning, building a database, data analysis, and outcomes and further work), the guide sets out a framework that details each project stage, the questions and tasks that need to be undertaken, and a series of additional points for consideration. The project planning stage is particularly useful as it assists local councils in contextualizing the project and defining the project scope, including identification of priority areas and unique or specific geographical features to be considered.

Steps

The four main stages are as follows:

- Project Planning
- Building a Database
- Data Analysis
- Outcomes and Future Work

Each section is supported by a summary table to identify subtasks, key questions, and data requirements along with useful pointers and further points for consideration.

Expected Results

- Understand key issues and approach to preparing LCLIP.
- Increased awareness of current vulnerability to weather events
- A LCLIP can deliver the following evidence:
  - Schedule of consequences of weather events
  - Analysis of important variables
  - Summary of discussion and commentary on significance of consequence, performance, and preparedness

Resources

Data collection is the primary area that may be resource intensive and has the most limitations as some data may not be readily available.

The website provides a suggested 10– to 12-week timeframe to prepare an LCLIP. Factors that will determine scope include local area geography; data availability; and priority sector areas, if any.

Sustainability

Greater understanding of local area and identification of expected/anticipated change over time support adaptation planning, opportunities for green infrastructure, and priority investment planning.

Pointers for Implementation

A complete LCLIP Pack has been prepared and is available via the website. The pack includes support materials for each of the four steps of the LCLIP process.

Reference

The tool can be accessed here: http://www.ukcip.org.uk/lclip/

Examples

Numerous UK case studies are provided on the website.

[16] http://www.ukcip.org.uk/lclip/

The Risk, Uncertainty and Decision-Making Framework

Tool: The Risk, Uncertainty and Decision-Making Framework	United Kingdom Climate Impacts Programme (UKCIP)

Objectives

The risk framework is a step-by-step process that aims to evaluate the most suitable adaptation measures.

Approach

The tool has been developed on standard decision-making and risk principles and will assist users in answering the following questions:

* What climate change risks could affect a decision?
* What adaptation measures are required, and when should they be implemented?

The tool supports the decision-making process and reflects the iterative process of decision making and the interconnection between various stages of decision making. This is particularly relevant for adaptation planning as various options are assessed at various stages and the monitoring process enables a feedback loop to be incorporated. This framework therefore embeds a cycle of review within decision making.

Steps

* The process is detailed as follows:

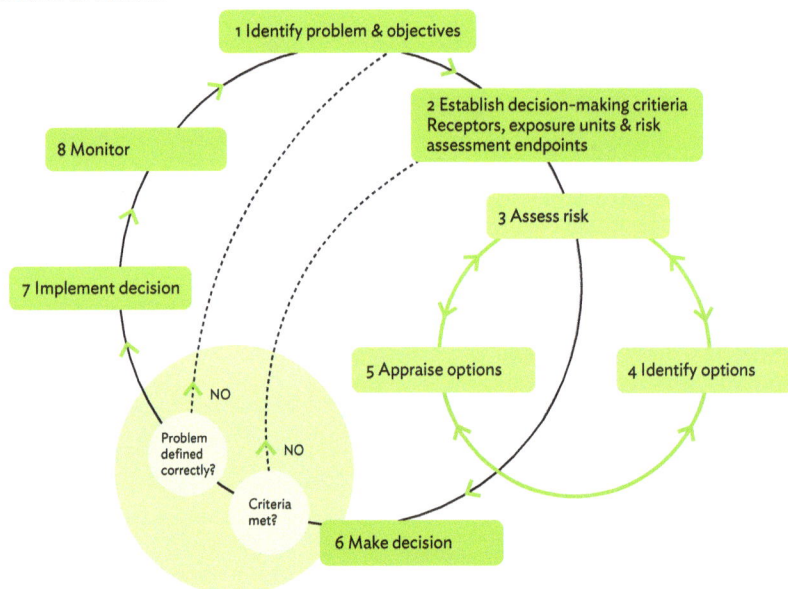

Expected Results

* Decision making informed by assessment of risk and established monitoring and evaluation framework.

Resources	Sustainability
No specialist requirements. Time-based inputs.	Responds to the iterative nature and adaptation planning and provides a framework to capture change

Pointers for Implementation

The technical report that sets out in detail the development of the framework and the rationale and guidance for each step can be downloaded and used as reference document.

The tool provides a conceptual framework for approaching adaptation planning at an institutional and/or business/personal level. It complements the Adaptation Wizard tool (see Subsection 4.10.1).

Reference

The tool can be accessed here: http://www.ukcip.org.uk/risk/

Examples

Numerous UK case studies are provided on the website.

Guide to Climate Change Adaptation in Cities

Tool: Guide to Climate Change Adaptation in Cities	The World Bank

Objectives

This guide provides leaders and practitioners working in developing and transitioning economies with practical insights on climate change adaptation. In addition to the explanation of the key climate change adaptation principles, the guide relates these principles to the challenges faced within informal settlements, the urban poor, and other vulnerable groups.

Approach

Structured in eight chapters, this guide provides a concise and accessible summary of climate change adaptation. The guide includes:

- Introduction
- Climate change impacts on cities
- Framing adaptation in cities
- Developing a roadmap for adaptation
- Informal settlements, the urban poor, and other vulnerable groups
- Sector-specific adaptive responses
- Financing adaptation in cities
- Conclusion

The guide reflects an integrated development approach and covers many crosscutting issues. In particular, Chapter 6 details sector-specific responses while highlighting interrelationships with other areas and issues.

Steps

Not specifically a tool kit that includes step-by-step instructions or detailed "how to" sections, this reference document can be read as a whole or by individual chapter to improve understanding of climate change adaptation issues in cities.

Expected Results

- Improved understanding of climate change adaptation in cities, including benefits of proactive policies, relationship between resilience and adaptation planning, poverty alleviation, and disaster risk reduction
- Improved understanding of climate financing
- Identification and understanding of crosscutting issues
- Awareness of available tools and additional relevant resources

Resources	Sustainability
Not applicable.	Crosscutting issues of disaster risk reduction, public health, economic development, and food security are all considered.

Pointers for Implementation

- The guide provides a good overview of crosscutting issues including health, poverty, resilience, green infrastructure, and urban service provision.
- Table 3.2 in Chapter 3 provides a concise and useful summary table that highlights differences and convergence between Disaster Risk Reduction and Climate Change Adaptation.
- Chapter 4 can be read as a stand-alone section to assist in the preparation of adaptation plans including performance indicators.
- Chapter 4 also includes a summary table of further assessment tools available at the city level.
- Chapter 6 provides sector-specific adaptive responses but is useful for summarizing and identifying crosscutting issues.
- Document cross-references the UK Climate Impacts Programme tools referenced in this tool kit.

Reference

The guide can be accessed here: http://www-esd.worldbank.org/citiesccadaptation/index.html

Examples

Worked examples, which are found throughout the document, include projects and case studies covering Brazil, Bangladesh, Malaysia, the Philippines, and several other countries.

The guide has a text box that highlights key terms, concepts, and issues.

4.11   Disaster Risk Reduction

Building Resilient Communities

Tool: Building Resilient Communities: Risk Management and Response to Natural Disasters through Social Funds and Community-Driven Development Operations	The World Bank

Objectives

The tool kit "Building Resilient Communities: Risk Management and Response to Natural Disasters through Social Funds and Community-Driven Development Operations" is designed primarily to help Task Teams on World Bank social funds and community-driven development (CDD).

Approach

The tool kit introduces the concepts and components of Community Based Disaster Risk Management (CBDRM) and their key relationship to the achievement of the development and poverty reduction objectives. The tool kit also provides guidance and examples from past and current social fund and CDD operations about the most effective ways to manage operational challenges in undertaking CBDRM activities, particularly in relation to the rapid mobilization and scaling up of emergency response operations.

Steps

The nine modules of the tool kit correspond to key thematic areas of CBDRM. Each module can be used separately or in combination with other modules.

- Module 1. *The Role of Social Funds and CDD Operations in Disaster Risk Management* introduces the main concepts and components of CBDRM and provides an overview of current trends in disasters, with a specific focus on climate change. It includes information on hydrometeorological and geological natural hazards, but none on biological disasters, as this topic is covered in other thematic areas of the World Bank.
- Module 2. *Integrating CBDRM into the Project Cycle* offers guidance on incorporating disaster risk management, using community-based approaches, into the World Bank's country programs and social funds/CDD projects in countries at high risk of natural disasters. Guidance is provided on community-level risk assessment, specifically tools and methods for conducting multihazard risk analysis and hazard, vulnerability, and capacity assessments to inform the development of country programs and social funds/CDD projects and subprojects.
- Module 3. *Disaster Risk Reduction (Prevention, Preparedness and Mitigation)* gives an overview of the main principles of CBDRM, with a particular focus on disaster risk reduction (DRR). Potential DRR areas for social funds/CDD operations are outlined, including capacity building of government and communities to plan and implement CBDRM activities, structural and nonstructural measures to mitigate disaster risks, diversification of livelihoods, risk financing and transfer methods, and adaptation to climate change.
- Module 4. *Disaster Response (Rescue and Relief) and Early Recovery* focuses on immediate postdisaster response and early recovery. It summarizes key issues and actions that may be taken by social funds/CDD operations to help government manage and coordinate disaster response with the full and active participation of affected communities, such as emergency needs assessments, vulnerability/gender targeting, and beneficiary communications.
- Module 5. *Longer-term Disaster Recovery (Rehabilitation and Reconstruction)* discusses key issues in longer-term postdisaster recovery. The range of forms and methods for social funds/CDD operations to deliver recovery assistance are described, specifically the restoration of communal assets, livelihoods, shelter/housing, and natural resources. The module also provides guidance on the integration of recovery programming into regular social funds/CDD operations (that is, existing strategies for emergency operations).
- Module 6. *Monitoring and Evaluation* outlines some of the key challenges in measuring the performance of CBDRM programming. Information and Examples are provided on the development of results-based performance frameworks at the project and subproject levels (including objectives, expected results, and performance indicators).
- Modules 7, 8, and 9. *Gender in CBDRM, Focus on Disability, Focus on Older People, Children and Minorities* provide an overview of particular needs and capacities of each group and highlight the risks and consequences of excluding these groups. Modules include actions to increase inclusiveness.

Tool: Building Resilient Communities: Risk Management and Response to Natural Disasters through Social Funds and Community-Driven Development Operations

The World Bank

Expected Results

- Improved disaster management
- Reduced vulnerability
- Integrating social aspects with disaster risk reduction

Resources

- Data collection is required.
- Focus on community-based planning, and long-term capacity building will require sustained resource support.

Sustainability

- Community-based and community-driven responses can be cascaded into wider city/government-level plans.
- Engagement with high-risk communities supports green city development through increased education on appropriate land use siting, support to livelihoods, and increased preparedness/resilience to natural disasters.

Pointers for Implementation

- Modules 2 and 3 are particularly relevant to green city planning, highlighting crosscutting issues and suggesting ways to integrate key concepts across wider government/city level plans.
- The conclusion of each module includes a guide to further references.
- Annex 2.1, Annex 3.1, and Annex 3.2 all provide useful tools for undertaking rapid assessments and engaging the community.

Reference

The tool kit can be accessed here: http://siteresources.worldbank.org/INTSF/Resources/Building_Resilient_Communities_Complete.pdf

Examples

Six case studies covering Honduras, Indonesia, Madagascar, Malawi, and Pakistan are provided.

Cities and Flooding

Tool: Cities and Flooding: A Guide to Integrated Urban Flood Risk Management for the 21st Century	The World Bank

Objectives

The guide provides forward-looking operational guidance on how to manage the risk of floods in a quickly transforming urban environment and changeable climate.

Approach

The guide takes a strategic approach to managing flood risk, in which appropriate measures are assessed, selected, and integrated into a process that both informs and involves the full range of stakeholders. Illustrated with more than 50 case studies, a series of "how to" sections, and a set of guiding policy principles, the guide embodies state-of-the-art integrated urban flood risk management. Comprehensive and user-friendly, the guide serves as a primer for decision and policy makers; technical specialists; central, regional, and local government officials; and concerned stakeholders in the community sector, civil society and nongovernment organizations, and the private sector.

Steps

The resource has seven chapters, each of which can be read as a stand-alone section or as a whole. The guide is structured as follows:

- Understanding Flood Hazard
- Understanding Flood Impacts
- Integrated Flood Risk Management: Structural Measures
- Integrated Flood Risk Management: Nonstructural Measures
- Evaluating Alternative Flood Risk Management Options: Tools for Decision Makers
- Implementing Flood Risk Management
- Conclusion: Promoting Integrated Urban Flood Risk Management

Expected Results

- Increased awareness and understanding of flood hazard and impacts
- Understanding of structural and nonstructural interventions
- Application of integrated flood risk management techniques
- Preparation and integration of flood risk management principles into urban planning frameworks

Resources

The guide is aimed at policy and decision makers and not intended to be resource intensive.

Technical studies may be identified during scoping studies of local areas that will require additional technical expertise: hydrologist, civil engineers, urban planners, and economists.

Sustainability

Reflects integrated and risk-based land use planning principles and provides detailed examples of these in practice.

Pointers for Implementation

Each chapter concludes with a "how to" section that sets out the main steps to guide policy development, develop interventions, and manage implementation. Each chapter also provides a complete bibliography should users wish to examine any issue in more detail.

References

The resource can be accessed here: https://www.gfdrr.org/urbanfloods

The guide is available in English, Indonesian, Spanish, and Russian.

Examples

The reference guide provides more than 50 global case studies demonstrating key principles and practice.

Building Urban Resilience: Principles, Tools, and Practice

Tool: Building Urban Resilience: Principles, Tools, and Practice	The World Bank

Objectives

The handbook is a resource for enhancing disaster resilience in urban areas. It summarizes the guiding principles, tools, and practices in key economic sectors that can facilitate incorporation of resilience concepts into the decisions about infrastructure investments and general urban management that are integral to reducing disaster and climate risks.

Approach

Integrated urban planning and risk-based planning principles are adopted in the handbook. The handbook has three main sections:

- Principles of Urban Resilience
- Tools for Building Urban Resilience
- The Practice of Urban Resilience

The handbook reflects a logical and analytical methodology for users to apply.

Steps

The handbook is a reference resource. Individual chapters can be accessed, as required, to provide overall guidance and/or to address a specific issue.

Expected Results

- Increased understanding of sector relationships, planning and financing investment in urban areas, and how this "builds" resilience
- Increased understanding of systems-based approach to urban management
- Increased application and use of tools profiled
- Incorporation of concepts into urban programs and projects
- Better definition and understanding of risks facing cities and management response.

Resources

The handbook is aimed primarily at planners and practitioners to help improve knowledge and shape intervention responses. However, it is relevant for decision makers and community representatives to improve technical knowledge and understanding of issues.

Sustainability

Reflects systems-based, integrated, and risk-based land use planning principles and provides case study examples of practice. Importantly, the handbook links these principles and issues to finance considerations.

Pointers for Implementation

Look for the case studies and good practice boxes throughout handbook.

Each chapter commences with a summary of key points, provides key resources,and concludes with comprehensive reference and further reading list.

Chapter 2 includes a series of "checklists" against specific actions. These prompts complement Steps 1 and 2 of this tool kit well.

Reference

The handbook can be downloaded for free via the World Bank e-library:http://elibrary.worldbank.org/doi/book/10.1596/978-0-8213-8865-5

Examples

Case study examples are provided in each chapter, highlighting good practice and application of key concepts and approaches.

How to Make Cities More Resilient: A Handbook for Local Government Leaders

Tool: How to Make Cities More Resilient: A Handbook for Local Government Leaders	United Nations International Strategy for Disaster Reduction (UNISDR)

Objectives

To assist local government leaders and policy makers in preparing and supporting public policy, decision making, organization, and implementation of disaster risk reduction and resilience activities

Approach

Structured in three main chapters and supported by detailed annexes that provide the necessary technical tools to assist users in "making their city more resilient."

- Why Invest in Disaster Risk Reduction
- What are the 10 Essentials for Making Cities Disaster Resilient
- How to Implement the 10 Essentials for Making Cities Disaster Resilient

Steps

Chapter 2 sets out 10 essential components:

- Essential 1: Institutional and Administrative Framework
- Essential 2: Financing and Resources
- Essential 3: Multi-hazard Risk Assessment–Know your Risk
- Essential 4: Infrastructure Protection, Upgrading and Resilience
- Essential 5: Protect Vital Facilities: Education and Health
- Essential 6: Building Regulations and Land Use Planning
- Essential 7: Training, Education and Public Awareness
- Essential 8: Environmental Protection and Strengthening of Ecosystems
- Essential 9: Effective Preparedness, Early Warning and Response
- Essential 10: Recovery and Rebuilding Communities

Expected Result

- Understanding of key requirements and concepts to develop a resilient city
- Preparation of public policy that actively addresses disaster risk and resilience

Resources

As a learning tool, resources associated with individual's time to read and discuss each section.

Specific interventions and approaches/application of tools with an overview of key strategies and actions needed to build resilience to disasters.

Sustainability

Practical guidance and consideration to crosscutting issues relevant to city/municipal government. The progression from theory to practice/application is extremely relevant for policy and decision makers.

Pointers for Implementation

Annex 1 provides a self-assessment framework for local governments to undertake. This section complements Step 1 of the green city tool kit.

Annex 4 provides a comprehensive and current list of available tools and resources. These references include a general guidance section and balance sheet provided in line with each of the 10 essential items.

References

The handbook can be downloaded for free via UNISDR website: http://www.unisdr.org/campaign/resilientcities/toolkit

Examples

Supporting the handbook, the UNISDR Making Cities Resilient: My City is Getting Ready website offers relevant additional resources: http://www.unisdr.org/campaign/resilientcities/

4.12　Green Infrastructure

Green Infrastructure—Valuation Tools Assessment

Tool: Green Infrastructure – Valuation Tools Assessment	Natural England

Objectives

To assist users select most appropriate tool to enable valuation of green infrastructure providing relevant information on the gaps and areas for further work.

Approach

An assessment of current tools used to value green infrastructure, including a description summary and explanation of how to use respective tool, identifying gaps and areas for further work.

Steps

A reference document that requires users to read and consider how it may be relevant with its application to a particular city.

Expected Results

- Increased understanding of available green infrastructure and associated tools to determine value
- Understanding of application limitations, e.g., context and transferability, access to data, etc.
- Understanding of functionality of green infrastructure and relationship to integrated planning and ecosystem services

Resources	Sustainability
Not applicable	Linking urban infrastructure requirements with green development outcomes (green infrastructure) and ecosystem services

Pointers for Implementation

The report is largely aimed at a United Kingdom audience. However, the methods and tools summarized can be adapted for Asian cities. The detailed summaries of each tool set out how the original intent of the tool and how it has been modified (if applicable). From here, it is possible to consider application in Asian cities.

Reference

A publicly available and free report that can be accessed from Natural England website: http://publications.naturalengland.org.uk/publication/6264318517575680

Examples

Does not provide worked examples but highlights each tool assessed.

4.13   Urban (General)

Eco² Cities

Tool: Eco² Cities: Ecological Cities as Economic Cities	The World Bank

Objectives

The World Bank initiative Eco² Cities provides a conceptual framework for developing green and sustainable principles into practice. The initiative includes a comprehensive book that sets out key issues, current practice, opportunities, and limitations. It is supported by the Eco² Cities Program, which aims to provide more detailed guidance to move principles to practice.

The Eco² Cities Program approach has four guiding principles:

- A city-based approach
- An expanded platform for collaborative design and decision making
- A one system approach
- An investment framework that values sustainability and resiliency

Approach

Each section or component, as highlighted in the figure below, is addressed in detail in a corresponding chapter. To demonstrate points and also to support users prepare plans based on sustainable principles, the guide includes exercises for users to complete. It also includes a series of checklists and where to find additional resources.

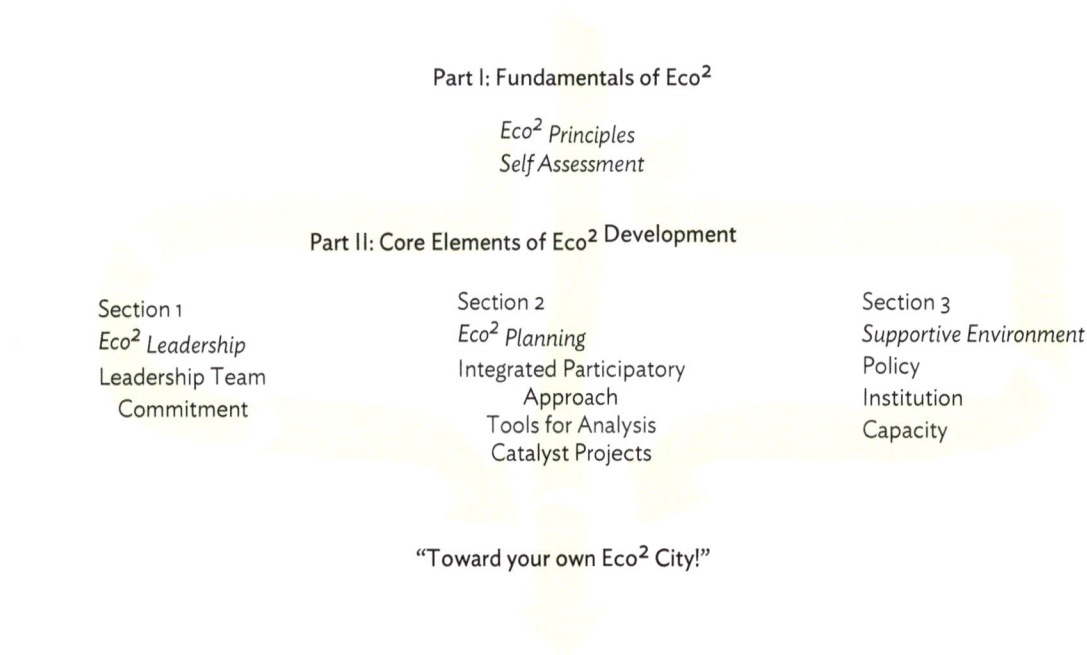

Part I: Fundamentals of Eco²

Eco² Principles
Self Assessment

Part II: Core Elements of Eco² Development

Section 1
Eco² Leadership
Leadership Team
Commitment

Section 2
Eco² Planning
Integrated Participatory
Approach
Tools for Analysis
Catalyst Projects

Section 3
Supportive Environment
Policy
Institution
Capacity

"Toward your own Eco² City!"

Tool: Eco² Cities: Ecological Cities as Economic Cities — The World Bank

Steps

The above figure highlights the framework and process of Eco² and represents the steps or elements for developing sustainable city development plans.

Each section provides a detailed step-by-step guide supported by worked examples and case studies.

Expected Results

- Integration of Eco² principles in urban planning and urban management practice
- Enhanced masterplans and investment plans
- Improved governance and awareness within government

Resources

Reference document supports policy makers, technical staff, and decision makers. No specialist resource other than individual time.

Sustainability

A city approach or systems approach is consistent with current sustainability principles and approaches that recognize the interrelationship between sectors and different elements of the city or urban area.

Pointers for Implementation

- Chapter 2 (see Table 1.1) provides a summary table of key principles and suggested "stepping stones" to support implementation. These stepping stone principles are then cascaded and reflected at the conclusion of each subsequent chapter thus signposting users to key issues and possible responses.
- Part 3 of the reference documents includes "sector notes" that introduce urban sectors and provide a concise summary of key issues and emerging themes.

References

The document can be accessed here: http://siteresources.worldbank.org/INTURBANDEVELOPMENT/Resources/336387-1270074782769/Eco2CitiesBookWeb.pdf

Additional supporting resources can also be found on the Eco² Cities website: www.worldbank.org/eco2

Examples

Detailed case studies are provided in Part 3 and include examples from developed and developing countries.

Liveable Cities

Tool: Liveable Cities: The Benefits of Urban Environmental Planning — United Nations Environment Programme (UNEP)

Objectives

To provide a comprehensive overview of the benefits integrating environmental management into urban planning and urban management. Its principal aim is to provide readers with practical examples and tools demonstrating how environment and urban planning can be integrated. Commencing with an outline framework to urban environmental planning, and followed by identification and explanation of several instruments/tools that can be employed to achieve integration.

Approach

The document provides worked case studies to demonstrate the use, benefit, constraints, and other practical observations in the use of

- Integrated Development Planning
- City Development Strategies
- Eco City Planning (ecoBUDGET), a proprietary tool developed by the International Council for Local Environmental Initiatives (ICLEI—Local Governments for Sustainability)
- Strategic Environmental Assessments

Tool: Liveable Cities: The Benefits of Urban Environmental Planning	United Nations Environment Programme (UNEP)

Steps

The document sets out an overall framework to achieve integration and highlights what tools/steps are available within a framework that characterizes each instrument within the following:

- Policy Instruments
  - Information
  - Voluntary
  - Economic
  - Regulatory
- Process Instruments
  - Baseline studies
  - Participatory methods
- Planning Instruments
  - Environmental Profiles
  - SWOT (strengths, weaknesses, opportunities, and threats) analysis
  - Ecological footprint assessment and Strategic Environment Assessments
- Management Instruments
- Environmental budgets and audits

Expected Results

- Understanding of benefits and relationships between well-managed urban environment; economic development; and other crosscutting issues of health, poverty, security, and resilience.
- Understanding of urban environmental planning
- Understanding of lessons learned from other countries and how green city planning can be improved or further developed

Resources

Time for users of document

Sustainability

Conceptual framework and introduction to key principles provides sound basis for green city planning and development. Supports the principle adopted in this tool kit, which states that establishing basic urban environmental infrastructure is key to green city development.

Pointers for Implementation

Annex 2 provides the following example tool kits that can be adapted.

- Sustainable procurement
- Checklist for visioning conference
- Guides and programs that focus on Participation
- Structuring and Environmental Profile
- SWOT Analysis
- Steps in Rapid Ecological Footprint Assessment
- ecoBUDGET Phases

Reference

The document can be accessed here: http://www.unep.org/urban_environment/PDFs/LiveableCities.pdf?bcsi_scan_97e98328e2b67804=0&bcsi_scan_filename=LiveableCities.pdf

Examples

Annex 1 provides a comprehensive list of case studies from eight countries.

Asian Green City Index

Tool: Asian Green City Index	Economist Intelligence Unit and Siemens

Objectives

To provide an assessment methodology to enable Asian cities to be ranked according to the level of environmental/green policy and resultant impacts on environment and quality of life

Approach

This sector-based tool approach with the methodology of selection includes the capital cities by size and by importance, with the index divided into eight categories and 29 individual indicators. Data collection was made by publicly available official sources and 22 cities were clustered into groups which defined by population size, area, income, density, and temperature.

Steps

1. Selection
2. The index
3. Data Collection
4. Indicators
5. Index construction
6. Clusters

Expected Results

- The reference document concludes by ranking cities within five categories: Well above average, above average, average, below average, and well below average.
- Understanding of performance indicators that can be used for measuring green cities.

Resources

Developing an index that is country or geography specific will require data collection and management.

Sustainability

Provides a global benchmark that can be used as a basis for developing performance indicators relevant to alternative geographies. Consideration to crosscutting themes, such as health and/or quality of life, access to alternative modes of transport, and green jobs, should be made.

Pointers for Implementation

Provides a possible framework for developing index and performance criteria. Also includes quality of life measures, some of which cross over with other city indexes. This document can be provided as conceptual framework to develop other indicators that may be used to develop an index.

Reference

The document can be accessed here: http://www.economistinsights.com/sites/default/files/downloads/Asian%20GCI%20FINAL.pdf

Examples

The document showcases and examines 22 cities representing a combination of capital cities and leading business centers. These can be found from page 36.

Sustainable Planning Tool Kit

Tool: Sustainable Planning Tool Kit	International Council for Local Environmental Initiatives (ICLEI—Local Governments for Sustainability)

Objectives

To provide local government staff and decision makers with the necessary tools and guidance to develop, prepare, and implement sustainability plan.

Approach

The tool kit provides

- Step-by-step guidelines for how to achieve each milestone
- Tips on what to include in a sustainability plan
- Best-practice examples
- Checklists and templates
- Guidelines for organizing a team of experts to develop the plan

Steps

The tool kit is structured around the five major steps:

- Milestone One – Conduct a sustainability assessment
- Milestone Two – Establish sustainability goals
- Milestone Three – Develop a local sustainability plan
- Milestone Four – Implement policies and measures
- Milestone Five – Evaluate progress and report results

Expected Results

- Local Plan
- Policies and Measures
- Progress and report of the results

Resources	Sustainability
Membership to ICLEI required.	Provides a platform to establish baseline information that can be used during Phase 1 of the city assessment.

Pointers for Implementation

This resource is only available to ICLEI members.

Relevant documents that are publicly available include

- 10 Keys to Sustainability Planning Success
- What is a Sustainability Plan

Reference

The tool kit can be accessed here: http://www.icleiusa.org/action-center/planning/sustainability-planning-toolkit

Examples

Not available

E-resources

Tool: International Council for Local Environmental Initiatives (ICLEI – Local Governments for Sustainability)	Online reference

Objectives

To build and serve a worldwide movement of local governments to achieve tangible improvements in global sustainability with specific focus on environmental conditions through cumulative local actions.

Approach

ICLEI's first global programs were Local Agenda 21, a program promoting participatory governance and local sustainable development planning, and Cities for Climate Protection™ (CCP), the world's first and largest program supporting cities in climate action planning using a five milestone process including greenhouse gas emissions inventories to systematically reduce emissions. ICLEI's programs and campaigns looked beyond mere environmental aspects and embraced wider sustainability issues. The ICLEI Council acknowledged this and formally broadened the mandate of the association in 2003, renaming the association ICLEI–Local Governments for Sustainability.

Summary of Resources

The website is a vast repository of information and practical guidance across the following thematic areas:

- Resilient city
- Biodiverse city
- Low-carbon city
- Resource-efficient city
- Smart urban infrastructure
- Green urban economy
- Healthy and happy community

However, many of the tool resources require users to be a member of ICLEI. This requires an application and annual fee to be paid. As such, the website has limited utility for nonmembers. For nonmembers, the website provides introductory remarks and explanation for all thematic areas and includes a series of accessible and downloadable case studies which are useful as reference and examples of good practice.

Expected Results

- Awareness of available resources and current and emerging good practice

Reference

The tool kit can be accessed here: http://www.iclei.org/home.html

References

Asian Development Bank (ADB). 2010. *Sustainable Transport Initiative Operational Plan.* Manila.

————.2013. *Investing in Resilience: Ensuring a Disaster-Resistant Future.* Manila.

————.2012b. *Key Indicators for Asia and the Pacific 2012: Green Urbanization in Asia.* Special chapter. Manila.

————. 2011a. *Urban Operational Plan 2012–2020.* Manila.

————.2012a. *Handbook on Poverty and Social Analysis: A Working Document.* Manila.

————.2013. *Asian Water Development Outlook 2013: Measuring Water Security in Asia and the Pacific.* Manila.

————.2012c. *Green Cities.* Manila.

Asian Development Bank (ADB). 2014. *Urban Climate Change Resilience: A Synopsis.* Manila.

A. Cotton. 2000. *Tools for Assessing the O&M Status of Water Supply and Sanitation in Developing Countries.* World Health Organization.

A. K. Jha, T. W. Miner, and Z. Stanton-Geddes, eds. 2013. *Building Urban Resilience: Principles, Tools, and Practice.* Directions in Development. Washington, DC: World Bank.

A. S. Gupta. 2009. *Guidance Notes on Services for the Urban Poor: A Practical Guide for Improving Water Supply and Sanitation Services.* Water and Sanitation Program, World Bank.

A. Peal, B. Evans, and C. van der Voorden. 2010. *Hygiene and Sanitation Software: An Overview of Approaches.* Water Supply and Sanitation Collaborative Council.

B. Madsen, N. Carroll, D. Kandy, and G. Bennett. 2011. *Update: State of Biodiversity Markets.* Washington, DC: Forest Trends.

B. Madsen, N. Carroll, and K. Moore Brands. 2010. *State of Biodiversity Markets Report: Offset and Compensation Programs Worldwide.*

Cities Alliance, United Nations Environment Programme (UNEP) and International Council for Local Environmental Initiatives (ICLEI). 2007. *Liveable Cities: The Benefits of Urban Environmental Planning.* Washington DC.

Cities Development Initiative for Asia. 2014. *City Infrastructure Investment Programming and Prioritization (CIIPP) Toolkit.* http://cdia.asia/wp-content/uploads/2014/09/CIIPP-toolkit-brochure.pdf

C. Lüthi et al. 2011. *Community-Led Urban environmental sanitation planning: CLUES - Complete guidelines for decision-makers with 30 tools.* Dübendorf: Swiss Federal Institute of Aquatic Science and Technology (Eawag) / Geneva: WSSCC / Nairobi: UN-HABITAT.http://www.susana.org/en/resources/library/details/1300

C. Lüthi, A. Morel, E. Tilley, and L. Ulrich. 2011. *Community-led Environmental Sanitation Planning: CLUES. Complete Guidelines for Decision Makers with 30 Tools.*

C. Lüthi, A. Panesar, T. Schütze, A. Norström, J. McConville, J. Parkinson, D. Saywell, and R. Ingle. 2011. *Sustainable Sanitation in Cities—A Framework for Action.* Sustainable Sanitation Alliance (SuSanA) and International Forum on Urbanism (IFoU).The Netherlands: Papiroz Publishing House.

D. Bongardt, F. Creutzig, H. Hüging, K. Sakamoto, S. Bakker, S. Gota, and S. Böhler-Baedeker. 2013. *Low-Carbon Land Transport: Policy Handbook.* Routledge.

D. Dodman, D. Brown, K. Francis, J. Hardoy, C. Johnson, and D. Satterwaite. 2013. *Understanding the Nature and Scale of Urban Risk in Low-and Middle-Income Countries and its Implications for Humanitarian Preparedness, Planning and Response.*

D. Grey and C. Sadoff. 2007. Sink or Swim? Water Security for Growth and Development. *Water Policy.* 9 (6). pp. 545–571. IWA Publishing.

D. Rodriguez, C. van de Berg, and A. McMahon. 2012. *Investing in Water Infrastructure: Capital, Operations and Maintenance.*

Department for International Development. 2011. Practice Paper *Guidance on using revised Logical Framework.* London.

Economist Intelligence Unit and Siemens. 2011. *Asian Green City Index: Assessing the Environmental Performance of Asia's Major Cities.*

H. Suzuki, A. Dastur, S. Moffatt, N. Yabuki, and H. Maruyama. 2010. *Eco^2 Cities: Ecological Cities as Economic Cities.* Washington, DC: World Bank.

J. Eichler, A. Wegener, and U. Zimmermann. 2012. *Financing Local Infrastructure – Linking Local Governments and Financial Markets.* Deutsche Gesellschaft für Internationale Zusammenarbeit (GIZ) GmbH.

M. Lindfield and F. Steinberg, eds. 2012. *Green Cities.* Manila: Asian Development Bank.

M. Palaniappan, M. Lang, and P. H. Leick. 2008. *A Review of Decision-Making Support Tools in the Water, Sanitation, and Hygiene Sector.* The Pacific Institute and The Environmental Change and Security Program.

M. S. Westfall and V. A. De Villa. 2001. *Urban Indicators for Managing Cities.* Manila: Asian Development Bank.

Natural England. 2013. *Green Infrastructure – Valuation Tools Assessment.*

N. Carter, R. Kreutzwiser, and R. de Loe. 2005. Closing the Circle: Linking Land Use Planning and Water Management at the Local Level. *Land Use Policy.* 22. 115–117.

P. Gleick, M. Palaniappan, and M. Lang. 2008. A *Review of Decision Making Support Tools in the Water, Sanitation and Hygiene Sector.*

P. Rode and G. Floater. 2012. *Going Green: How Cities Are Leading the Next Economy: 3GF Edition.* London, UK: LSE Cities.

R. Brown, N. Keath, T. and Wong. 2009. Urban Water Management in Cities: Historical, Current and Future Regimes. *Water Science and Technology.* 59(5).pp. 847–855.

S. Angel. 2012. *Planet of Cities.* Cambridge, MA: Lincoln Institute of Land Policy.

S. Joss, ed. 2012. *Tomorrow's City Today: Eco-City Indicators, Standards and Frameworks.* Bellagio Conference Report. London: University of Westminster.

S. Lehmann. 2010. *Green Urbanism: Formulating a Series of Holistic Principles.* S.A.P.I.EN.S [Online], 3.2 | 2010, Online since 12 October 2010, Connection on 10 October 2012. URL : http://sapiens.revues.org/1057

S. Moffatt, H. Suzuki, and R. Izukuka. 2010. *Eco² Cities Guide: Ecological Cities as Economic Cities.* Washington, DC: World Bank.

S. Naumann, M. Davis, T. Kaphengst, M. Pieterse, and M. Rayment. 2011. *Design, Implementation and Cost Elements of Green Infrastructure Projects.* Final report to the European Commission, DG Environment, Contract no. 070307/2010/577182/ETU/F.1, Ecologic Institute and GHK Consulting.

S. Reed, R. Friend, V. Toan, P. Thinphanga, R. Sutarto, and D. Singh. 2013. *"Shared Learning" for Building Urban Climate Resilience – Experiences from Asian Cities.*

The World Bank. 2013. *Planning, Connecting, and Financing Cities Now: Priorities for City Leaders.* Washington, DC.

UN-Habitat. 2011. *A Practical Guide for Conducting Housing Profiles.* Nairobi, Kenya.

————. 2012. *Urban Planning for City Leaders.* Nairobi, Kenya.

UNEP. 2012. *Application of the Sustainability Assessment of Technologies Methodology: Guidance Manual.* Nairobi, Kenya

United Kingdom Climate Impact Programme (UCKIP)

United Nations Human Settlements Programme (UN-Habitat), UNEP, and ICLEI. 2010. *Sustainable Urban Energy Planning: A Handbook for Cities and Towns in Developing Countries.* Nairobi, Kenya.

www.ingramcontent.com/pod-product-compliance
Lightning Source LLC
Chambersburg PA
CBHW041120280326
41928CB00061B/3467